CW0076l999

GODDESSES
AMONG
US

Book 1

KIMBERLY ANDERSON

New Life Clarity Publishing

205 West 300 South, Brigham City, Utah 84302

http://newlifeclarity.com/

Printed in the United States of America

ISBN- 9781087861920

Dedication

This book is dedicated to all the Goddesses out there – including you. If at times you feel lost, lonely, overwhelmed or afraid, and are looking to change your life, this book is for you.

Your power lies within you dear one.
Strength and passion burn within you.
Healing is at your fingertips. Within you
is the Goddess you are meant to be.

Stand Tall and Unleash Your Inner Goddess.

Table Of Contents

About The Author

Kimberly Anderson

Kimberly Anderson is an Intuitive Transformational Coach and Business Creative. She is a Best Selling Author, Speaker & TV Show Host of 'Unleashed with Kimberly'. Her writing is featured in 'E The Magazine' and she frequently gets asked to be on podcasts and shows.

Kimberly helps women understand that their limiting beliefs and past experiences don't define them; they are lessons to build from. Teaching women to understand and trust their intuition is a profound tool in their success. Her inspiring stories of life experience and delightful humor shift people out of old beliefs and habits, to find inner wisdom and a positive energy flow. She helps to tap into and pull out innate gifts and talents, which helps women out of being stuck and inspires them to create the businesses they've always dreamed of.

Kimberly has created her signature 3 part series of the 'Unleash Your Inner Goddess' to encourage girls and women of all ages to step into their brilliance, ending with a not to be missed 'Goddess Retreat'. Her exclusive private and group coaching programs are for future thought leaders and professionals, like herself.

Kimberly C Anderson ~ Founder/Owner of Aphrodite Enterprises Inc. w: KimberlyACoaching.com e: Support@kimberlyACoaching.com https://www.facebook.com/AphroditeEnterprisesInc/ https://www.linkedin.com/in/kimberly-c-anderson/

Introduction

It is an honor to introduce you to 16 consciousness leaders in the first book of the series, *Goddesses Among Us.* These women have stepped into their power and are inspiring others by speaking their truth.

These ladies are friends, sisters, aunts, mothers, daughters, grandmothers and neighbors. Just like you, they are Goddesses Among Us. They have overcome an abundance of trauma, obstacles, negativity, limiting beliefs and adversities. They have graciously stepped into the spotlight to share their powerful stories with us in these inspirational, and at times, heart wrenching conversations.

Each of these women are a blessing to humanity. May we follow in their light, learn from their experiences, and bring their wisdom into our lives.

These transformational conversations bring to light that we all go through "stuff". We are all on journeys of experience, change, choice, and transformation. Take the profound wisdom and enlightenment found in this book to help you on your journey of life and in your own transformation.

I am grateful to all of the women in this book. It is a true honor to help share their stories. May the words in this book bless you with wisdom and divine energy, to your higher consciousness and expansion.

Kimberly Anderson

CHAPTER 1

Trauma to Transformation

Abbey Sweeny

Domestic violence is the leading cause of injury to women - more than car accidents, muggings, and rapes combined. In the US, a woman is assaulted every nine seconds. For two years, I was physically, sexually, financially, and emotionally abused. I was left broke, and broken, forced to move back in with my parents and restart my life. All my belongings, heirlooms, and gifts from others were lost. For so long, I thought life as I knew it was over, and that I was just simply waiting for my life to end.

After a failed attempt on my life, I realized I wasn't being punished. Instead, I was being given an opportunity. A second chance. It was then that I realized: a complete restart was not a bad thing. Rather, it was a chance to learn from my mistakes and live a different life. It was my time. Now, years after returning home, I have taken my situation and turned it into a business to help others and promote positivity to every individual, no matter what setbacks or misfortunes life has thrown at them.

abbey@asmotivational.com
http://www.asmotivational.com/

"Absorbing all the lessons she could, she transformed her trauma into purpose." ~ K.A.

Trauma to Transformation...Abbey Sweeny

Kimberly: I am super excited to introduce Abbey Sweeny. You've had quite the life journey so far. But first, please share who you are and what you do.

Abbey: Well, I'm actually a Marine brat. I grew up in a very regimented home. My brother followed suit and went to the same college as my dad. It's funny - my entire family became engineers, and then I was this artist who was so full of emotion. I went through two years of very aggressive domestic violence, and when I got out, I had one of those moments where I realized I had two options; I could either continue moving in a positive direction, or I can just stay where I was and take my own life. In my mind, those were my only two options. But I loved my family, so suicide definitely wasn't the answer.

I knew I needed to figure myself out. So I started taking steps towards improving myself. I went to therapists, psychologists, psychiatrists, I talked through a lot of issues, but I felt like none of these doctors were helping. I ended up hiring a life coach, and I could feel there was a real connection between us. I stayed with her, and we spent twelve weeks together, working on me. That was probably one of the most transformative periods of my life. Working with her made me realize what I wanted to do with my life: I wanted to be a life coach.

I started my own coaching business, and I followed her 12-week model. I changed some of the steps to fit my particular emphasis, which is working with people who are struggling to overcome trauma. Domestic violence is mostly what I focus on, because that's where I have a personal connection. I help survivors and victims, as well as abusers. I also help ex-convicts who were arrested on domestic violence charges. A lot of their trauma has nothing to do with domestic violence. The 12-week process works for both. Fast forward to today, and I speak with clients on an international level. I'm honored to be able to spread the good word about recovery.

Kimberly: What an incredible story. So you help not only the survivors of domestic violence, but the abusers as well.

Abbey: That's right. We can continue to treat the symptoms all we want. The symptoms are traumatized survivors, both men and women who have left abusive relationships feeling worthless. And yes, I treat survivors, but I also focus on the people committing that abuse. If they haven't received some form of treatment, most abusers are more than likely to abuse again. My goal is to give them the proper treatment in order to prevent further abuse from occurring.

Kimberly: I love that. I totally understand what you're talking about. When it comes to domestic violence, it doesn't matter who you are, what you look like, or where you are in the economic world. It is literally a global issue, it's happening all over the world, and I love that you are stepping forward and speaking about not only the survivors, which is massively important, but the root cause. I think that's amazing.

I love what you're doing and, I'm happy that you're in this space as well. But what would you say has been one of your biggest obstacles you've experienced, and how did you overcome that obstacle?

Abbey: Well, actually making the decision to leave my abusive relationship definitely wasn't a big challenge. It was one of those situations where I told him I was leaving, and he literally said, "Fine, I'm done with you." I had nowhere else to go, so I moved back in with my parents.

I would say the largest obstacle I had to overcome was deciding if I should actually kill myself or not. That was a big one. I didn't think my life was worth living. I only attempted once, and thankfully I wasn't successful. But I think I needed to make that attempt, you know, because I needed to learn that suicide was not the answer.

I had gone to a psychiatrist, because at the time, I had really great medical insurance through Tri-Care. I think I only saw him for about three weeks, because it just wasn't working. The therapist was doing no talking. None whatsoever. So I left him and went to another one who was a female. I hoped she might be different, but I just got the same reaction from her. She, just like the first, wanted me to do all the talking.

It just didn't feel like this whole therapy thing was working out. I left those appointments feeling even worse than when I walked in. So I decided, "Okay, I'm going to try something else." I just kept trying new things. I tried one psychiatrist, and he wanted to put me on Ambien. I told him there was no way I was going on any medication. I didn't need drugs - I just needed practices to put in place so I could get over my trauma. I knew I had the motivation to get better, but the doctors still kept pushing for me to take medication. Once I even got into a full-fledged argument with a psychologist over whether I was going to take medication or not.

I felt like someone was trying to control me, the same way I did when I was in that abusive relationship. I felt like no one was actually helping me. I decided to try something else, and just two days later, I found a life coach online who looked promising. I'm very metaphysical, and when I went in, I wanted to focus on that. Turns out that was her approach as well! So we started working together.

Kimberly: Oh my gosh, you've touched on so many things already. You went from this abusive relationship to your attempt to take your own life. That's incredible, to have these painful experiences, yet retain your determination to continue living and improving. Also, I find it interesting that all these therapists' knee-jerk reactions were to give you medication.

Abbey: Well, in his guy's defense, I was only sleeping about an hour a night at this time. Repressed memories were coming to me in the form of nightmares, so I just wouldn't sleep. During my relationship, my partner would slip me ketamine. He would drug me pretty aggressively, then I would be sexually assaulted. When I attempted to take my own life, I tried to overdose on medication my doctors prescribed. When I got my stomach pumped, the doctor said, "The only reason that this stuff didn't kill you is because your system is so used to this."

I explained this to the psychiatrists, I told them why I was so anti-medication, but they still wanted to put me on some form of sleeping meds. Needless to say, I never visited those doctors again.

Kimberly: I understand, and like you said, his reasoning behind wanting to give you Ambien was a knee-jerk reaction. He just wanted to give you a pill, instead helping you figure out why you weren't sleeping.

Abbey: Oh yeah. During that relationship, my days' time was so sad because I wasn't making any money, and I had $50,000 of credit card debt in my name. I was swimming in that, plus car payments, medical bills, and I was constantly living with the fact that I wasn't good enough, or so I believed. And then at night, when I fell asleep, all I dreamt about was sexual assault, over and over and over again.

Kimberly: It's an amazing journey that you've been on. Can you talk a little bit about what helped you start working through this trauma?

Abbey: The first thing I did was set aside time and space. When I moved in with my parents, I went from living in a four-bedroom home to a studio apartment. All of my stuff had to either fit in a box in the garage, or in this small room, so it wasn't really my space. I thought I would be out in a few months, so I didn't think it would be a big deal.

It's been two and a half years, and I still live with my parents. They're gone 80% of the time, so in a way, it almost feels like my house. I've taken over, they come to visit every now and then.

I used to sit in my room and feel so trapped by all of this stuff, and I didn't have much to begin with – I lost a lot of stuff. When I left, I really only grabbed what I could, but it was still so much. I didn't have a dresser, so all my clothes were everywhere, I felt there was no organization in my life. The first thing my coach advised me to do was to take a part of my little room, and create a sacred space.

I bought a turquoise plate, an incense holder with a candle holder, and I would just sit silently in front of it. This was my sacred space to set up my lights, light the candle, and when I sat there, all I could see was that space. After a little while of sitting in this space, I started noticing my perspective was shifting. Instead of feeling trapped, I decided to feel thankful.

I was thankful I actually had a house to live in. I started practicing gratitude in that space, and before too long, I reached a point where I didn't need to have that space anymore. I became so used to practicing gratitude that I could feel grateful anywhere. I could take those feelings with me wherever I went. I didn't need to sit in a special corner of my room to feel thankful. Instead of being upset that I was 23 years old and living with my parents, like I said, I just felt grateful to have a roof over my head. I felt thankful to have parents who loved me, clothed me, and fed me. I started feeling thankful for small things I was used to taking for granted.

Instead of believing I was entitled to a different life, or a different living situation, I started accepting what was. I started telling myself that I was getting exactly what I needed in each moment. That was the big change – taking that sacred space and narrowing it down to one idea: I have me, and I should be pretty freaking grateful for that.

Kimberly: Wow, so it was a perspective shift for you, because it allowed you to focus solely on that small candlelit space, and when you were comfortable and ready, you turned the lights on and acknowledged the rest. That's so powerful. I love that.

Abbey: Well, I'm a visual learner, so if I can see it, it bothers me. If I have a pile of clothes in the corner, it bothers me. My boyfriend now is wonderful, but he is such a messy person. I'll do his dishes before we go to bed, and he asks me why. Well, because if I can see it, it's going to bother me! That's who I am. He's an auditory learner, so for him, he has to say things out loud, or he'll write them down on a mirror with a dry erase marker. We just learn in different ways, which is absolutely fine.

Kimberly: It's interesting when you pick up on how we learn, especially visual people who don't do well with the auditory methods of learning.

Abbey: I have an auditory processing disorder. That was another truth about myself I had to accept. I also have ADHD, so when I listen to podcasts, I can only listen for about five seconds, and then I can't listen anymore because my brain doesn't comprehend it. I really try and incorporate my practices with the Universal Design principles in mind. I want my practices to be used universally.

Kimberly: That's an amazing tip. You've got some incredible wisdom to share with everybody. It's important to have these tools under our belts. One of the things I always talk about – which you've touched on – is sitting in gratitude, because that is such a mind shift. Once you do that, your perspective will start changing instantly.

Abbey: In Buddhist tradition, there's a necklace they wear with over one hundred beads on it. One form of meditation is to go through and for every bead, name one thing you're thankful for. Well, I don't have a necklace, but I make that list in my head. I mentioned that I have ADHD. I have a hard time sitting in silence because my mind just doesn't stop, so for me to just sit completely still feels like a pretty big accomplishment.

Usually I can only achieve that calm state of mind after yoga, when I'm too exhausted to think about much of anything. When it comes to a thankfulness practice, there's a way you can slip into a form of meditation by picking a topic to be thankful for. For example, you can choose to feel grateful for having a roof over your head, and then you can dive deep into that gratitude:

"I'm thankful for this house, I'm thankful for the people who built it, I'm thankful for their parents who created them, I'm thankful for their education, I'm thankful for the trees that gave their lives for this house, I'm thankful for the painters," and so on. When you do that, you're really tapping into an unlimited well of gratitude.

Kimberly: I often teach gratitude meditation, because again, the mind doesn't shut off. The mind doesn't like to go blank; it's always thinking about something. So when we meditate, we think we have to be quiet and not think anything, and that's when the panic sets in. We're so used to thinking about something, and then those thoughts snowball into all these other thoughts, and you're just like, "Oh my God, I'm doing this completely wrong." So to sit in absolute gratitude and fee; grateful for everything, even the sound of birds chirping outside your window, can be a very powerful experience.

Abbey: And I think breathing has a lot to do with that meditation, too. Breathing has a lot to do with yoga, but just getting oxygen to your brain is helpful. I used to listen to meditation music that had a three-four-time signature, because it helped me breathe in and breathe out. It would flux just enough to remind me to keep my breathing the same, and I could meditate for hours, sweating like a hog and but not craving water because I'm getting all the oxygen I need just from breathing.

Kimberly: So powerful. Awesome wisdom. So, one of my other favorite questions to ask during these interviews is, if you could give your younger self one piece of advice, what would it be?

Abbey: "Hold on tight!" That would be my advice. Everyone asks me if I could go back and do it all over again, would I? And I can say, wholeheartedly, I would one hundred percent do it again. I would live my life the exact same way, because that's what got me to where I am today, and today, I am happier than I've ever been, at any other stage of my life.

After I left my ex, I was dating this firefighter who was big and buff. My ex was five-foot-five. Real short for a man. My ex was always an angry kind of guy, and once, after the breakup, he had come up to me and was trying to start a fight. My firefighter walked up behind me, and I just told him no. I told him I could fight my own battles now. He stepped aside. Then I looked my ex square in the eye and I just said, "Thank you." He didn't know what to do. I continued: "Thank you, because I'm so happy, I'm in such a happy place right now, and it's all because I had to overcome you."

I often think back to that moment. It was a turning point for me, to be able to look at this guy who strapped me to the front of his car and drove me around town, and thank him for it. I made it very clear to him I wasn't reinforcing how he treated me. I just calmly let him know I wasn't going to hold on to that anger anymore. I thanked him for putting me through all that. I thanked him for showing me I could become so much more than what I was with him. There's absolutely nothing about that relationship I would change. Younger Abbey can listen to that. Just hold the hell on, girl! It's going to be a crazy ride, but you'll get through it.

Kimberly: I love it. I think it's important to look back at your younger self and know that if she saw you today, she would be proud. You've been awesome. Thank you so much for sharing your story.

Abbey: Thanks for having me, and thank you so much for giving us a platform to tell our story! If there's anything I can do to help people, I'll do it. That's my sole purpose.

CHAPTER 2

Audacious Confidence

Alicia Couri

Alicia Couri is the Audacious Confidence Growth Expert. As the RedCarpetCEO™, she strives to influence, edicate, inspire, and entertain her audiences. She is an Empowerment Speaker, a Kolbe Certified™ consultant, PI certified consultant, founder of Alicia Couri Inc & RedCarpetCEO™, the co-founder and executive producer of Dreamaniac TV. She is an author, actor, beauty and personal branding expert. She is the reigning Mrs. Elite United States Woman of Achievement 2020, as well as a multiple-award winner from the Woman of Achievement Organization. She was named one of the 100 Influential Women by the Boys & Girls Club of America for 2018.

Alicia has appeared on ABC, CBS, NBC, multiple radio shows and podcasts; she stars as the lead in multiple independent films, and she's a best-selling Amazon author. Alicia's mission is to help leaders step into their "Audacious Confidence," to live a life without limits. She's the founder, creator, and host of a live multi-streamed web show called the Audacious Confidence Show.

As a corporate consultant, Alicia develops leaders. She helps executives properly align business goals with personal performance. She focuses on elevating confidence, reorganizing teams to reduce stress & conflict, ensure the right people are in the right seats, and promote an overall happier work environment that is both highly productive and profitable for her clients.

#1 Audacious Confidence™ Expert
www.alicia360.com
Alicia Couri Inc - Kolbe Certified™ Consultant
Founder, Executive Producer & Host DramaniacTV

"She overcame negative beliefs and discovered grace and beauty within herself." ~K.A.

Audacious Confidence...Alicia Couri

Kimberly: I am so excited to introduce Alicia Couri. I've already read your bio, but please, share more about what you do.

Alicia: Thank you so much, Kimberly. I am so excited to be here. I strive to influence, educate, inspire, and entertain. Whatever I do - whether I'm speaking, consulting, coaching, acting, or hosting my web shows on DreamaniacTV - whatever I do, it falls within one of those four categories, or sometimes all 4 of them.

I love doing what I do. I've been doing this for decades. I'm 50 now, and as confident as I am now, I didn't always feel that way. Early on, I really struggled with my own self confidence. And even though I knew there was a lot inside of me to contribute, I held myself back. I held myself back because I was afraid of being judged by others. What would they say, you know? What would they think? Can I really do this? I didn't think I was enough; I don't think I was pretty enough, smart enough, etc. So, I had a coach come in and really help me uncover all those limiting beliefs that were holding me back. All those things in my bio happened, most of them in the last five years. So it's important to unleash your inner goddess, to really understand who you are and what you are meant to do. It's essential to find out what your purpose, your passion, and your dreams and goals are. Stop keeping them bottled up inside, and start releasing them.

I only did the pageant last year because when I was in my teens and twenties, I didn't think I was pretty enough. I definitely wasn't tall enough, and although I was a flight attendant, I was just too afraid to step out and do anything like that. Even though people often said, "Oh, you'll win and you'll feel great," I still didn't believe it. I would never even try to step out and do anything like that. And then at 50, I was like, "What the heck? Let me take this leap, and do this thing," and I won! Look at what can happen when you shift your confidence. My platform, Audacious Confidence, strives to help you become bold and confident. I had to learn how to step into that confidence. And that's what I teach other people to do now: to step out and find their confidence.

Kimberly: I love that. I love the name, too.

Alicia: Audacious Confidence.

Kimberly: It's intentional, and I think the power lies within that. I agree with everything you said. Often we hold back because of our own limiting beliefs, but look at what you're doing now! Once you were able to conquer those beliefs, you were unstoppable. That's so powerful.

Alicia: And it's not always obvious what your limiting beliefs are, which is why sometimes you need a coach or a mentor to help you see your blind spots. You won't see your blind spots until you become more aware of your actions.

Sometimes when you see yourself doing something, you can stop yourself and say, "Wait a second, that's an old pattern, that's an old belief, why am I doing this?" And then you have to become self-aware enough to actually do that. That only comes through coaching and mentoring. I now believe I am more self-aware than I used to be. I've developed a process called the Seven Steps to Audacious Confidence. Last night on my show, I interviewed my beautiful friend Megan Fenyoe. We were talking about how she's the "I AM Enough" girl and I'm the "Audacious Confidence" girl, and sometimes we catch ourselves not listening to our own advice, so we have to go through our own processes again, in order to regain confidence in ourselves. We're all works in progress, none of us are perfect, and we have to learn to forgive ourselves in order to move forward.

Kimberly: That is absolutely true. It's interesting, because self-awareness means having all those tools in your toolbox.

You can go, "Hey, wait a minute, that's an old belief. That's not me anymore. I am good enough, I can be audacious, I am audacious," and doing that really shifts that power back to you.

Alicia: Absolutely. When I was building my brand around confidence, I looked for a word to amplify the word "confidence." Since my initials are AC, I was looking for an A word because confidence was the C. I felt like I needed something that's AC, because I was building the brand AC everywhere. My makeup & hair business was AC Beauty. So it made sense to look for A words to go with Confidence, and I finally came up with the word audacious. I did a sample test with some people I knew, and my friend said, "That word does not suit you at all. That word is not you." I asked her why she thought I couldn't be audacious.

The problem was, she was thinking about the word in a negative context. People tend to think that someone who is audacious is insufferable, or overbearing. When I really started to dissect that word, I knew it defined me. Audacious means to be bold and daring, and that's who I used to be as a child before I started developing all these negative beliefs about myself. I looked back at myself as a three-year-old child, and I was bold enough to say whatever was on my mind. Everyone knew I was that kind of girl. So I decided to be that girl again. I started owning the word "audacious," and I started developing my own courage to step out and do things I would normally avoid, like participating in that beauty pageant, for example.

Kimberly: Awesome! I love that you can sit there. confidently, and share all these fears with us. What would you say is one of the biggest obstacles you've faced, and how did you overcome that obstacle? I know we were talking already about negative beliefs, that's a huge one, and it's crippling for many people.

Alicia: The thing about negative beliefs is that they stack. I think the biggest challenge I faced was believing I was beautiful. And people look at me when I say that, and they're like, "How could you not believe? I mean look at you!" Well, it took me a long time to get to where I can look at myself in a mirror and appreciate who I was, and not just outward beauty. Internal beauty, too.

I was so insecure on the inside. I didn't like anything about myself, and it took a long time to believe in my own beauty.

It took going back to that three-year-old child. After age three, things changed for me. I was born in Trinidad, and when I was four and a half years old, my family moved to Australia. This was in the 1970s. I went to a school that was predominantly white, and when I say predominantly white, I mean the darkest person in the school was I think from India. It was a university town. My father actually attended university there. There were people from all different places, but my sister and I were the darkest kids in this school of 700 or more children. They'd never really seen people with my skin color. And I'm darker than my sister. They'd never seen anyone with my hair texture, our accents, or anything like that.

I had to revert back to that three-year-old child I was, in order to understand the genesis of those limiting beliefs. Kids used to ask questions like, "Why is your nose so wide? Why are your lips so big? Why is your hair so curly? Why is this part of your hand lighter than this part of it? Do you taste like chocolate?" And I just got tired of people asking these ignorant questions, so I just started shutting down. I was five years old, and that was the only way I knew how to respond.

Another challenge was that I never had a representation of beauty that looked anything like me. You know, beauty in that culture was straight hair, blonde hair, blue eyes, tall and thin. Not that I wasn't thin, I was always a skinny little thing, but I was short. I hated my height, I hated my skin color, I hated my hair texture, my accent, the way I spoke, the way I looked. Everything. I used to put a clothespin on my nose at night to try and straighten it out. I would go to sleep with that clothespin on my nose. It's no wonder why I'm claustrophobic as an adult.

My whole life, people have been telling me I was pretty, but I didn't see it. I couldn't see it. I didn't think there was a concept of beauty I could fit into. So that was, I think, the biggest hurdle I had to overcome. I had to learn how to look at myself in the mirror and tell myself I was beautiful. The more I started doing that, the prettier I became, and the more I believed in my own beauty. Before then, I never took pictures of myself. I hated how I looked. I used to run from cameras. Anytime I saw a camera, I would duck and dodge it, because I hated the way I looked in any picture. Now I take pictures all the time, and I love the way I look, because now I fit into a concept of beauty that I have created.

Kimberly: Amazing. It's interesting to see how you've carried that simple concept into adulthood.

Alicia: Without recognizing it.

Kimberly: Those negative beliefs are truly crippling. That's why I talk about it. That's why I try to help people understand that a negative belief is just that. A negative belief. Not a fact. It's just an idea that's been reinforced over and over again.

Look how deep you had to go in order to find those positive beliefs. It didn't just happen overnight, and it certainly wasn't easy, because those were deep-rooted negative beliefs you've been carrying around. The power they held over you is just unbelievable.

I'm curious; during these early childhood years, after you came home from school, were you talking to your parents? Were you asking them these same questions?

Alicia: No, I felt like they didn't have the answers, either. I thought if they had the answers, they would have told me.

Kimberly: You're beautiful, and I would imagine your mom is too. So for you to not look at Mom and think, Well, my mom's pretty, and look up to her for that, is a really interesting thing.

Alicia: Yes. Wow. It never occurred to me to look at my mom as an example of beauty. I never thought of that; I just looked at everything else that was portrayed on television and in the magazines.

Kimberly: Now, I know you said you had a coach and so forth, but what was it that finally helped you realize that it was those things from way back when, that were causing these negative feelings in the present? How did you get through that?

Alicia: A couple things. Number one: I was in the beauty industry for 15 years, doing hair and makeup. As soon as a client sat down in my makeup chair, they would talk about all the things I needed to fix. I started to notice them complain about not feeling beautiful enough. I always tried to give them pep talks, to point out their positive features. I tried to focus on the parts I could really amplify, so that when they looked in the mirror after I was done, they would feel amazed, and proud.

That kind of started nudging me to start looking at myself the same way, to start noticing my own positive features, but I didn't fully recognize they were trapped in the same negative mindset I was. Through coaching them, I was also indirectly coaching myself to start acknowledging my own beauty, both inside and out.

Part of my journey to uncovering my own limiting beliefs came while I was coaching. I hired a coach, and I participated in a program to start building a stronger brand for my business better. What I didn't know at the time, was that it would eventually become a personal branding course.

My coach started asking about me, not business, and at first, it didn't make sense to me. But through that process of opening up and starting to understand who I was and what my story was, I started building my brand. I worked through Dr. Phil's Self-Matters. In the book, he talks about self-concept. One chapter asks the reader to recall ten defining moments in your life. To do that, I had to go back in my mind and dig up these defining moments that shaped me into who I was. I also had to name the beliefs that created those moments, as well as list five pivotal people and seven critical choices.

Doing those exercises really helped me dig deeper into the past. Those ten defining moments could be either positive or negative, but they weren't all negative. Some were very positive.

Kimberly: It's interesting that you stepped into the beauty industry, even though you felt so negatively about yourself.

Alicia: God led me right where I needed to be.

Kimberly: I love when we start recognizing things in people because we're teaching them, we're coaching them, we're being their biggest cheerleaders. Just like you were doing, when you had your clients in the chair and you're like, "No, you are beautiful," and being able to transform them. I did makeup artistry too, so I totally understand what you're talking about. When you transform someone just with makeup, their energy changes, everything changes, so for you to even witness that, and know you helped foster that change, I would think your own mindset would begin changing, too.

Alicia: It started giving me confidence in my own abilities, but I still didn't value what I did, because I just felt like anybody could do it. I honestly thought it wasn't a big deal; it just felt like I was slapping on some lipstick, blush, and some shadow. So what? I continued to devalue my own abilities, all these feelings were playing out in my actions and behavior. If you're doing something, and you don't value it, you'll devalue yourself. I have found, especially with women, we devalue ourselves. I would listen to someone's sad story and not charge as much as I normally charged, because I wanted to help them out. Instead, what I was doing was devaluing myself and what I had to offer.

I questioned myself. I started asking why I kept giving discounts, why I kept undervaluing my work. It didn't make sense. If you added up the travel costs, the costs of all the products and everything, I was coming out with a deficit on this deal. So I really had to stop and think about what I was doing, and why I kept giving it away, practically for free. This wasn't just a hobby, this was my business.

That's when I really started digging into my own sense of value. I asked myself more questions: What do I value about myself, and why? Why am I placing someone else's value above my own? Why was I trying to prevent myself from earning a living? I was a hot mess. Hopefully my mess can help you.

Kimberly: It is. I appreciate the wisdom you're imparting. It's so important to have these conversations, and to really understand where those negative feelings come from.

Alicia: You have to dig it up. You have to start recognizing your own patterns. Then get the tools, because it's not something you can just willpower your way out of. You have to have tools to help you work through it. You need to understand what's happening, what's going on, and then say, "Oh, let me pull out this tool because this is what's going to help me." It's like trying to dig a trench with a table fork. A table fork's not going to get you very far. You need to use the right tool for the right job. And the only way you can do that is through education, understanding, and learning.

Kimberly: Absolutely. Now my last question: if you could tell your younger self one piece of advice, what would it be?

Alicia: There's so much I could tell her. I would go back and talk to my 16-year-old self, because at that time, I felt really bad about myself, like I wasn't enough. I felt that school was too difficult. Meanwhile my brother and sister were getting A's in all their classes, and I just felt like I didn't belong in this family. How could I be a part of it? I was creative, but my creativity wasn't appreciated in the same way academic achievements were. I couldn't get straight A's, and I was constantly beating myself up about it.

So I think I would go back to myself at that age and tell that young girl that she had so many other gifts, skills, and talents. I would tell her she hasn't even tapped into them yet. I would tell her to trust herself, because she had great intuition.

Kimberly: We could do an entire segment on the whole school system and creativity. But you reminded me of a quote, and I'm going to paraphrase because I can't remember exactly, but it's from Einstein. He basically says if you judge a fish by how well he climbs a tree, that fish is going to live its whole life thinking it's stupid.

Alicia: That's exactly it. You absolutely can't pigeonhole people and expect them to do well. That's why I do Kolbe. Kolbe is an assessment tool that is used to understand the cognitive part of your mind. That's where your instincts are, how you do what you do instinctively, how you are naturally wired to do it, etc. And sometimes we're like that fish trying to climb a tree – we're wired to do something one way, and when people tell us to do it another, we feel stupid. But when you do your Kolbe Assessment, you understand how you were naturally wired in your own way. That realization brings in so much grace, ease, and flow. You're really operating in your own zone of genius, instead of trying to do something the way someone else tells you.

Kimberly: So true and so powerful. When people realize they don't have to follow the norm, everybody's brilliant, and it's just a matter of time before you find out what you're brilliant at.

Alicia: And I'm still learning about myself! I'm still growing. I'm still enjoying the process of understanding the creative gifts that I have, and exploring them, instead of only limiting myself to working in the beauty industry. No. I can do so many different things, and I'm enjoying that process of discovery.

Kimberly: Yes! Creative types are all over the board, anyway. Alicia, it has been an absolute pleasure speaking with you today. I love your wisdom. You are stunning and beautiful, and I love that you're stepping out and becoming your audacious self. Thank you for being with me today.

Alicia: I appreciate you, Kimberly. Thank you for giving me this opportunity.

CHAPTER 3

Gifts, Words, and Underdogs

Amy Lanci

In 2018, after realizing her health coaching business was going nowhere, Amy Lanci finally decided to hang up her robes and step out into the world as a copywriter and marketing consultant. Within one week of switching everything over (her website, business cards, and brand), she hooked her first two clients. In that moment, she knew this was exactly where she was always meant to be.

Her love for words, as well as her gift for pulling stories has helped coaches, authors, healers, and speakers from all over the country hone in on their marketing message. In addition, she offers consulting and professional development training to corporations and organizations, with the goal of enriching their company culture and improving communication in the workplace. To Amy, this journey has been nothing short of magical.

http://www.amylanci.com

"Her ability to see the story within the story, and how she does it, is magic!" ~K.A.

Gifts, Words, and Underdogs...Amy Lanci

Kimberly: I am super excited to introduce Amy Lanci. I think your gift is amazing. Please tell us about what you do.

Amy: With small business owners, the hard part for them, and I can relate to this as well, is describing what it is they do. They have so many ideas, their minds are going off in so many different places at once, and my job is to sit down with them and help declutter their ideas. Then I help them figure out what their message is, and I take over writing the copy, or I instruct them how to write the copy themselves, if that's the approach they choose to take. I think the best way to describe what I do, is that my clients put all these words down, the words go through my head like an assembly line, and they come out more streamlined.

Kimberly: You're filtering it.

Amy: Yes, exactly

Kimberly: You have an amazing gift. But I think the story behind why you have that gift, and how you developed your ability to pull those stories out of people, is quite profound. So let's just dive into it. What has been one of the biggest obstacles you've had to overcome?

Amy: You know, I actually have two obstacles, and one of those obstacles led into the other. First of all, I was a speech-delayed child. Meaning, I didn't say my first word until I was three years old. And not only that, I was extremely shy. Extremely shy. I hid underneath tables in public. I clung to my parent's legs. I threw tantrums, especially if my family tried to take me to a family photo shoot. So that's why there aren't any professional family photos of us all together; I just would not go. My parents had me tested for autism. Not that there's anything wrong with being autistic, it's just that they didn't know what to do with me. My parents didn't think I was autistic, they just thought I was a late bloomer. Finally, after several years of speech therapy, I went on to become a straight-A student.

For whatever reason, I was always afraid of the world. I had very low self-esteem. When I was little, I spent so much time not fitting in. The only people I felt safe with were my family members. I felt a strong need to fit in with people, and this need cost me my individuality.

Which led to my next biggest obstacle: emotional eating. Rather than express my feelings, I started eating them. From second grade until well into college, my weight fluctuated. At age 24, I was diagnosed with nonalcoholic fatty liver disorder. That basically meant not only was I accumulating fat on different parts of my body (belly, arms, thighs), it also meant that my organs were starting to accumulate fat as well. My body was under a lot of stress, and the doctors told me if I didn't do anything about this, I had ten years until my liver started to scar, which is cirrhosis.

I went in to get my first liver biopsy. When you get a liver biopsy, you go in and there's a whole operating room filled with people. One person is holding the big needle, the others are monitoring you, and then this other person comes over with your IV drip and injects a painkiller. After they put the needle in, you have to stay in some room for five hours before they let you go. I'm just lying in the dark with the other patients, and I remember sitting there in the dark thinking about how I'm going in to get this biopsy, and my family doesn't even know about it.

I only told my then-boyfriend (who is now my husband), and maybe a couple friends. And all I could think of, as I lay there, was how I had brought this all on myself. That realization led me on this journey of not only healing my body, but healing my spirit as well.

And I heal my spirit through learning other people's stories. When I meet strangers at airports and bus stops, sometimes within twenty minutes, they're telling me their life stories. They tell me these private details about their lives, they tell me about their parents, and I always thought that was normal. I thought that was just how a normal conversation worked. It wasn't until recently that I realized that kind of thing wasn't normal, that most people don't like to get too personal too quickly.

Because it took me longer than most children to start speaking, I think I naturally became a good listener. I learned how to earn a person's trust. I became that safe space for them to share their secrets without judgment.

Kimberly: I love it. Now, you talked about not having that backbone, and I think back to your story of being a child, and going through speech therapy and stuff. How old were you when you started to actually have conversations? Did it happen quickly?

Amy: I think I was about four or five years old. It's interesting; as far as reading goes, I was a late bloomer there, too. I didn't start reading until second grade, but when I did, I could pronounce words more clearly and accurately than the other kids. A lot of kids were sounding words out, and I was just reading line by line by line by line. It seemed like once I got something, I got it. It was a long struggle to reach that point, but I believe that's just how I am. I'll keep working on something until I get it, and once I get it, I'm good.

Kimberly: That's really fascinating. What were some of the things that helped you during those difficult moments in your life, when you felt like you just were never going to grow a backbone?

Amy: I think being really close with my family helped. In Asian American families, you have very deep ties with your relatives. That helped. Also, just finding and making friends with other people I could trust. It took me a while to find people I could trust, people I felt safe with, but it happened. I recognize my people instantly now. I can see someone and I'll think to myself, Oh, you're my kind of person. I don't know why, and I don't know how I notice them, but I do, and I stick with them.

Kimberly: When you say you didn't trust people even as a child, which I think is really interesting, what was it that finally allowed you to start feeling like you could trust people again?

Amy: When I started trying to make friends outside of my household, I remember being very shy. During my first week of preschool, I was coloring some page in a coloring book, and I remember this one girl came by and she was snarky to me. She told me I was coloring outside the line, that I was coloring wrong. I instantly felt sad, like I'd just been humiliated and rejected.

But soon after that, another girl came up to me and said, "Don't listen to her." She told me I didn't have to color inside the lines. She and I became friends pretty quickly. She kind of, without realizing it, showed me it was safe to trust people outside of my household. When another person, especially someone who wasn't related to me, actually stood up for me, that was huge.

Kimberly: Wow. What a pivotal moment at such a young age. That's great you were able to recognize you could trust someone outside of your family.

Amy: Yeah. Interesting.

Kimberly: Now, as a child, you sat in observation, watching the world around you. You watched, you listened. And because you didn't speak, you were learning people's mannerisms; you were watching them, paying attention, even to how you are communicating your wants and needs to your parents, without actually verbalizing it. So it's really easy to see how those habits led you into a career in science, as well as writing.

Amy: It makes sense. Maybe spending my childhood as an observer helped. I allowed the other parts of my brain to develop in a slightly different way than it might have, if I had started speaking sooner. It's so funny, because for the longest time I didn't call myself someone who operated with both sides of the brain. I just called myself either a scientist, or a creative. But then recently, a friend reminded me that I did both; I'm both right-brained and left-brained. And it was the first time that I actually realized that.

Kimberly: So, if you could go back and give your younger self one piece of advice, what would it be?

Amy: I would tell her to hang on. Just hang on. "Everything's going to work out. I know it's hard, I know you're misunderstood, but everything you're struggling through now is going to pay off down the road."

Kimberly: I think it's important to sit down with ourselves, even at our age now, and tell ourselves that we're proud of them. You need to be able to look in the mirror and tell your reflection, "I'm proud of you."

Amy: Oh my gosh, we do. I was a health coach for a while. I tried to help people lose weight, and I remember so many people criticized themselves. They were so critical of their bodies and of themselves as people.

There was a period where I was going through my own weight loss journey. I was getting healthy, going to the gym, running on the treadmill, etc. And as I worked out, I would think about how my friend's father was overweight; the way he kept himself trim was by keeping an old photo of himself when he was heavier. He keeps it with him and looks at it when he needs an incentive to stay slim and not eat so much.

I just kept thinking about how I couldn't do that to my younger self. I was in tears on that treadmill, thinking about all this. I just realized that I never, ever wanted to disregard my past self, no matter what her flaws were. She deserves to be honored.

Regardless of how healthy or unhealthy I had been in the past, that person was still me. And if it wasn't for that version of myself, I wouldn't be who I am now.

Kimberly: That's such a great point. I love your story, and you've brought up some amazing points about embracing who you were, who you are now, and who you're going to be in the future. I just think that's a profound feeling.

Amy: Thank you. I'm just here to make sure that people have an outlet to tell their stories, including my own.

Kimberly: I've seen you work a room, and I want everyone to know that the ability that you have, to pull stories out of people, is magic. You take all that gargle, filter it, and turn it into a beautiful piece of art.

Amy: Thank you so much. I just love getting to the heart of what people say. That's really what I do. I'm so grateful for different platforms like this, for the events we've attended, and being able to share my gift with people.

Kimberly: We're always learning, expanding, and becoming more aware. I love it. I love your wisdom, and I love hearing about your journey. I can't wait to see where you go from here.

Amy: Thank you. Thank you so much.

CHAPTER 4

Find Your Inner Joyy

Burcu Onaranel

I was born and raised in Turkey. I followed society's rules until I finally had an epiphany and shifted my life. Before the shift, I earned a degree in business administration from Uludag University, then worked as a Human Resource Specialist in a large company. I lived a very comfortable life.

One day, I realized I was simply doing the same things day after day. I was not growing or learning. My soul was unhappy. I began self-improvement. I took NLP (Neuro-Linguistic Programming), became a professional life coach, and I followed the NLP Master Practitioner. During my training, I discovered my true passion. I wanted to be an inspirational speaker, own my own business and live in the United States.

In June 2016, I quit my job and left my life in Turkey behind to begin a new life in another country. I studied English, then completed my postgraduate program in Media & Global Communications and Digital Marketing. I began working with entrepreneurs, life coaches, authors, speakers, fitness coaches, etc. to improve their marketing and communication strategies.

I joined Toastmasters to improve my public speaking skills and became Vice President of Education for a chapter. I started attracting my own clients. In January 2019, I launched my own business, Joyy! Marketing and Coaching. I dreamt a life for myself and then I created it. Today, I am overjoyed to share my story to help people become the best versions of themselves.

At Joyy! Marketing and Coaching, we help entrepreneurs improve not only their businesses, but their personal lives, too. We work with passionate people dedicated to making an impact in the world.
www.joyyburcu.com

"She had to break through barriers, her heart's desire was to live with passion, and now she wants to help you." ~K.A.

Find Your Inner Joyy ...Burcu Onaranel

Kimberly: I am excited to introduce Burcu Onaranel. Burcu, I love the name of your company. Please talk a little about what you do.

Burcu: I am the founder of JOYY! Marketing and Coaching. At JOYY, we focus on our clients' feelings, wants, and desires, in order to help them reach their personal and professional goals. We have two different aspects of our business – one focused on marketing goals, marketing strategies, social media management, and the second aspect focuses on personal coaching. We help our clients tap into their inner joy. We want to help you discover answers to life's fundamental questions: Why am I here? What is my purpose in life? How does my business fit into my purpose?

Kimberly: You've done so well with branding. Every time I think or hear the word "joy," I think of you.

Burcu: My mission is to spread joy. I believe everything is dualistic, and I like to focus on the positive side of life.

Kimberly: What would you say is one of the biggest obstacles that you've overcome? And how did you overcome it?

Burcu: I grew up in Turkey, and I had reached a point where I could no longer live by my society's rules, as I understood them. I realized I had a choice in how I wanted to live my life and conduct myself. Most women, especially in the Middle East, understand this issue, because it's very hard to break those rules and follow your dreams and passions. I believe in order to feel truly fulfilled, everyone has to find out what their dream is, and then they need to take the necessary steps to achieve it.

I felt lost in Turkey. I hit bottom, as they would say in the 12-step program. I had everything I wanted in life - I had a good job, I had family, I had friends, but I still felt something was missing. It felt like my soul needed to come alive, and I wasn't feeling that back home. I needed joy, and I was deeply unhappy.

I just started doing my own research. I learned neuro linguistic programming (NLP), I started studying how the human brain worked, and my feelings began to shift. Through NLP, I discovered what I really wanted from life; I wanted to teach people. I felt called to move to the United States. Everyone I knew thought I was crazy, because I didn't know anyone in America, I didn't know English, but that didn't matter. I knew what I had to do, and four years ago, I left Turkey and moved out to California.

Kimberly: One of the words I associate with you, other than joy, is bravery. You had such desire burning within you. You left your home and came to the United States without knowing anyone, or even speaking the language. To me, that is a huge leap of faith. I'd love to hear more about that. It's just an incredible act of bravery. What were you thinking? What was going on in your mind as this was happening?

Burcu: At the time, I did not think I was being brave. Even now, I don't think I am brave, but when I look back at what I've accomplished, that bravery comes to light. Before I moved, it felt like my soul was on fire. It's so hard to put into words, but once I opened up and started taking chances, I was so excited about learning. I was excited to have new experiences. I would leave work on Friday night, feeling energized. When you are truly open, and you have faith, God helps you, the universe helps you, and it gives you the power to accomplish anything.

One of the techniques I teach is just to take things one step at a time. Take small steps. If you know something is wrong with your job, relationship, or whatever, the first thing you need to do is change your environment. It's not about quitting the job or leaving the relationship right away, but you have to take time to see your situation from a different perspective.

That's why I moved to America. I needed to change my environment. I knew I could no longer be happy where I was.

Kimberly: Did you have a place to stay, when you first arrived? Did toy come with some sort of plan?

Burcu: I had a plan. A friend of mine ran an agency that helps students travel to other countries for education, so I started from that angle. I knew I needed to learn English, so I decided to go as a student. I was placed in a home with six international students, and in the beginning, I struggled a lot. I lived with six strangers for over a year. That in itself was a huge adjustment, because I grew up as an only child. It was hard to share a home with that many different individuals.

Kimberly: I love your bravery. You uprooted yourself out of your home country, your family, your cultural identity, and left. Obviously, there was a lot of thought behind that decision, but it really demonstrates that you were willing to follow your dreams and become a beacon of light for others to follow. It's really wonderful that you're doing what you're doing.

Burcu: Thank you so much. It's tough, as you said. It is a huge challenge to leave your comfort zone.

Kimberly: It really is. People don't like to feel uncomfortable. We like to live in our own little bubbles, and in order to grow, you have to stretch yourself and step out of that comfort zone. And when you do step out, there are scary moments, but you learn to embrace that fear and do it anyway. There's no other choice. And you did that. You started that journey and created a whole new life. I think that is so awesome.

Burcu: Thank you so much. I appreciate it.

Kimberly: What was the hardest part of starting a new life? Was it leaving your family? Was it living with six other people you didn't know?

Burcu: I think seeing my dad cry was the hardest part. As I passed through the gate on the way to the plane, I looked back at him, and I was going to wave to him one last time, and I saw him crying. I was 25 years old at this point, and this was the first time I'd seen my father cry. And of course, once I saw that, tears started pouring from my eyes. I cried so hard I couldn't see. I questioned if I was doing the right thing, if this was the right choice. I wondered why they were letting me go.

Kimberly: Oh, you gave me chills. That moment was hard, but you were in full alignment with your destiny.

Burcu: I want everyone to be able to have a similar experience. I want everyone to follow their dreams. Even though, yes, there are tough times, but it's worth it. It's worth the struggle.

Kimberly: I love that. You're amazing, and I love the joy that you bring to people. Final question. If you could give your younger self one piece of advice, what would it be?

Burcu: I would tell my younger self to step out of her comfort zone, to challenge herself, and stay strong. Do what your heart tells you, and everything will be okay.

Kimberly: You have such an incredible story - switching countries, rebelling against your cultural rules, and then seeing your dad cry for the first time. Wow. How are your parents now? I know you kind of mentioned they're proud of you now, but were they always supportive?

Burcu: My dad transformed in a huge way. He really saw that I'm doing what I want to do, he saw that I am much happier here, and he supports me. My mom was always supportive because she lived abroad in Germany for eleven years, so she knows how it feels to leave home. She's very spiritual and supportive. But you know, family always wants you to stay with them. They still have this idea that I'll come back. Sometimes they'll even ask me when I'm going to come back home. But they accept what I'm doing. They've watched my transformation, and more than anything, they support me doing whatever is going to make me happy.

Kimberly: That's awesome. When you were talking, I realized you were actually the catalyst that helped your dad transform himself. That's another important thing to acknowledge. When we transform ourselves, we give others permission to do the same.

Burcu: Yeah.

Kimberly: I just think you're amazing.

Burcu: I'm having fun.

Kimberly: Thank you so much for sharing. Keep shining your light, because you do shine really bright.

Burcu: Thank you. This gives me the opportunity to share my story with everyone. I think you are amazing too. I'm so glad we did this together.

Kimberly: Thank you. Together, we can change the world.

Burcu: Thank you. Absolutely.

CHAPTER 5

Declaration

Darla Delayne

Darla Delayne is a master teacher and high-level coach with over thirty years of experience as an inspirational speaker. She helps women fine-tune their greatness and light up the world with the fires within. She pushes them to build and expand their business empires.

Darla's expertise in educational psychology served her well in multiple industries. She has conquered the business world while raising four children. She teaches women how to have it all, how to get exactly what they want.

Darla is driven by a need to inspire women to rekindle their power. In turn, their families, friends, communities, and countries all benefit from these empowered women. She believes when a woman is truly empowered and inspired, their decisions can truly make the world a much better place.

darla@darladelayne.com
https://www.darladelayne.com
https://www.facebook.com/darladelaynecoachspeaker

"For her, it was more than just a decision, it was a declaration, and that was when she truly found herself."
~K.A.

Declaration...Darla Delayne

Kimberly: I am so excited to introduce Darla Delayne. She is a truly amazing woman. Please, Darla; share a little bit about yourself.

Darla: Thank you so much. I am thrilled to be here. I work with women who either have a team, or are preparing to work with one. That's my area of specialty. For example, a realtor, a mortgage loan officer, or even a stager might have a team of people go into new homes and prepare them for viewing. So whether you're a business owner working with your very first group of employees, an entrepreneur with a VA working alongside them, or even someone in branding, I can help you. I've even got a history of working in direct sales, too. I do this by focusing on four key areas: time management, productivity, collaboration, and team building.

Kimberly: It's interesting. The more you help others, the bigger and better your business is going to be, and I think that's a very important thing to notice about what you just said.

Darla: Yeah. I've been in this industry for over thirty years. Almost forty years, actually. I was very young when I started - pretty much straight out of college. I was a teacher, and I taught for a couple of years. It was so easy for me. I realized I wanted other people to succeed. I wanted to teach them how to get what they wanted, and I knew I could help them get there.

I've worked with teams throughout my entire professional life, and I'm just trying to share what I've learned. You need to maintain a "give and receive" approach when you're working with a team, and if you're either giving too much, or taking too much, that might be why your team isn't functioning properly. Teamwork needs to be a true collaboration, which sounds obvious, but some leaders conduct their teams as if that wasn't true.

Kimberly: That's awesome. That's why you're such a great leader, because you recognize that. What was one of your biggest obstacles, either in your personal or professional life, and how did you overcome it?

Darla: I love this question. In my twenties, I was substitute teaching, and I was also working with different sales teams, and after work, I would come home exhausted, and that was pretty much it. My day was over. I was too tired to do much of anything. Plus, I was married, and I had my first child in my late twenties. But on my thirtieth birthday, I had this moment of clarity, where I felt like I hit rock bottom, and I stood up and decided I'm done. I decided I would never waste another day of my life. I wouldn't say everything I'd had had been a waste, but I truly felt as if I had not lived life and experienced everything I should have in my twenties. I had jumped right into a career without taking the time to explore life.

I decided to make some serious changes, and from there, oh boy, I didn't waste a moment. My thirties were full of fun and adventure. I got remarried. I had two more kids. My family moved like five times. I did all kinds of exciting things I never would have done in my twenties. Time was now very important to me. I was very aware of how fleeting time is, and as my fortieth birthday approached, I had another moment of clarity.

I realized I can do everything I want. No matter how busy my life was, there was a way to structure and organize my time to where I could do all these things that were important to me. And I had commitments, too: PTA, book club, raising four kids, etc. But I did it. I found a way to continue to live life, explore, and be productive.

However, in my early fifties, my life completely shifted. I got divorced, and that wiped me out, honestly. I now had a bunch of teenagers, I was a single mother, I had just started a real estate brokerage in Manhattan, etc. I was scared and overwhelmed all the time. We didn't have money for food, we were evicted; it really was such a crazy time period.

But I knew there was a way through it, and I knew it had a lot to do with my mindset. That's when I decided I was going to be happy, no matter what was going on in my life. Most things were outside of my control, but the one thing I could control was how I reacted to them.

That's how I became obsessed with mindset, how it affects our actions, and how those actions affect what materializes in our lives. Even when my life was chaotic, people would ask me: "How are you smiling right now? Why are you so happy?

Happiness is a choice. It's as simple as that. I can choose how long I want to suffer. I've discovered some tools that have helped me find happiness when everyone else would have thought I had no reason to feel happy. That was a real defining moment, when I came to that realization. All that turmoil and all that soul-searching led me into getting a life coach certification, which of course led me into the coaching field. I'd studied education and psychology and always loved that, but I always knew being a therapist wasn't my thing.

I've had many different types of businesses. I've been an actress, a producer, I've been a realtor, a stager, and I've been a teacher. Because I've done so much, my clients all feel reassured knowing that I understand their businesses. They know I know exactly what I'm doing, and that I can help them. When I talk about mindset, it's coming from a place of real experience, and my clients pick up on that. That's what gives them the confidence to work on themselves and change their own mindsets.

Kimberly: That's amazing. You connect with so many different people, and I'm finding that women are really stepping into their creativity.

Darla: Exactly.

Kimberly: That is so important, and it's a very powerful realization. We all feel this fear of stepping out there and doing something, but you're saying it's okay to give yourself permission to try things.

Darla: I'm glad you said that. We often feel as if we need to get that permission from someone or something outside of ourselves, but in reality, that permission comes from the inside. That's where our true power lies, and once we give ourselves permission to try things, we feel that power. Now, we are in charge of our lives. This is what I'm trying to do: to teach women that their power comes from the inside.

Kimberly: That's really powerful.

Darla: As women, we need to learn there's nothing to be afraid of. When we step up and take action, it's okay; there's nothing frightening or dangerous about it. It's a good thing. All we're doing is shining in our own way, and trying to change the world for the better.

Kimberly: Right. Exactly.

Darla: I have three sons and a daughter, and I've had these conversations with them where I encourage them to follow their passions. That wasn't something I did, early in life. I didn't follow my passion. It took me a while to finally start doing that, so I wanted to give my kids permission to follow their passions, so to speak. I wanted to let them know it was okay.

Kimberly: That's awesome, encouraging your children to follow their dreams. That really is the key to finding true happiness.

Darla: Absolutely. Many people, particularly women, just do things because that's what they think they should be doing. They do things because someone else told them that's what they were supposed to do. But they aren't following their passions. They aren't following their hearts, and that's all I try to encourage my clients to do. You need passion to run a successful business, and I help my clients discover their passion. I've helped several people find their path, and it's been incredible.

Kimberly: That's huge.

Darla: Yeah. You have to decide what you really, really want, and then you have to follow through. And you can't make excuses. You can't give up just because you've encountered a few obstacles along the way. Every obstacle is an opportunity for personal growth, and that's where working on your mindset comes in. You have to change how you respond to challenges.

Kimberly: It's so simple, yet so difficult.

Darla: Definitely. Our brains are programmed to work and think in a certain way, and it's just a matter of learning how to reprogram.

Kimberly: I love the work you do. I can feel your passion really shining through.

Darla: I'm so excited right now. I can't even tell you how much. I love it.

Kimberly: You know, going back to these moments where you were like, "Okay, it's sink or swim right now," and then making that decision and overcoming those obstacles with a new mindset – that really propelled you forward and put you on the path to success.

Darla: Right.

Kimberly: So, it all goes back to giving yourself permission and changing your mindset. I love that.

Darla: Exactly. And I don't want other women to wait until they hit rock bottom, like I did. Don't wait to make your own personal declaration.

Kimberly: I love that you call it a declaration. You're switching the energy, the perspective, and the belief surrounding it, and that is powerful.

Darla: Exactly. "Declaration" does have a different energy, doesn't it? There's a feeling of power behind that word.

Kimberly: If you could give your younger self one piece of advice, what would it be?

Darla: If I could tell teenage Darla anything, I would tell her, first of all, that everybody loves her. Even if they're not showing it. Every person loves, that's just what we do, but if they're not showing it, that's because something's going on with them.

Secondly, I would tell her to stop searching for everyone else's approval. Like we mentioned earlier, approval and acceptance comes from within. When I was younger, I was a people pleaser, and I completely gave my power away. What other people think about you and what you do is none of your business. What you think and how you feel about yourself is your business. I used to be so needy, so desperate for others' approval, and all it did was take away my joy. Don't get so wrapped up in someone else's approval that you sacrifice your own joy. That's what I'd tell young Darla.

Kimberly: I love it. There's so much power in what you're saying. I think your story is amazing, and I'm so grateful you were willing to share some of your wisdom. Thank you so much.

Darla: Thank you for having me. As I've said, I have such an appreciation for you stepping up and shining in this way. All the women involved in this project are incredible, and you're doing a great service for the women who are one day going to see this.

CHAPTER 6

Twice Deleted

Erica Palacios

Erica is the creator/producer of Twice Deleted Podcast. She is a Transformational Breath® Facilitator/Group Leader, and she provides occupational therapy services to children with disabilities. Her world was shattered when her 25-year-old daughter experienced a crippling mental health crisis. At the suggestion of a shaman, Erica began her journey of going within. She dedicated herself to supporting her daughter's healing, which ultimately led to Erica's own journey of healing and self-discovery. Through Transformational Breath® work, Erica became aware of her own negative beliefs, while at the same time confronting repressed childhood emotions.

Over time, Erica began trusting herself and her intuition, and she started relying on her faith. She let go of grief and guilt, and ultimately forgave both herself and others, creating a positive space for her daughter to heal. She is rich with insights into the inner workings of her heart and mind.

Strengthened by her journey from despair to hope, Erica is on a mission to share her story and increase awareness about mental health challenges. She is dedicated to helping parents understand the critical role they play, not only in their own healing and transformation, but in their children's mental transformation as well.

Erica@twicedeleted.com

"After realizing she had an inner connection with her spirit, she used her intuition to guide her." ~K.A.

Twice Deleted...Erica Palacios

Kimberly: I am super excited to introduce Erica Palacios. Erica, please share a little about who you are and what you do.

Erica: I do a couple things. I host a podcast, and the intention of that podcast is to increase the public's awareness about mental health issues. I want to highlight the role a parent can have in healing their child, whether the child is young or all grown-up. I'm trying to share the spiritual or energetic side of mental illness. So that's one thing that I do.

The other thing I do is I provide transformational breath facilitation for folks who are looking to bring more joy, meaning, and more overall happiness into their lives. We all want to feel good and experience moments of joy, and breath work is a very powerful tool in achieving a sense of wholeness. Those are the two things I focus on, other than my day job, where I work as an occupational therapist.

Kimberly: That's awesome. One of the things I love about breath work is that we kind of do it automatically. We do it without realizing it, so to really tap into the power of that is profound.

Erica: Yes. A lot of times, we shut down our breath, and as children, in order to keep ourselves from crying, we have to hold our breath. It causes us to block our feelings, as well as decrease our ability to breathe fully and properly. Through my breath work exercises, you're opening your respiratory system, and also discovering yourself at the same time.

Kimberly: It's pretty amazing. You could also make the argument that as adults, if we're holding back tears or trying to keep ourselves from saying something, we're holding our breath. So in a way, we are constantly holding our breath when we shouldn't, and suppressing our feelings can cause a lot of problems.

Erica: Yes it does, and we're really starting to understand that the physical and energetic body are interconnected. If we have unresolved feelings, such as fear or grief, those feelings leave an energetic signature, which in turn lead to mental health issues or even physical maladies.

Kimberly: Alright, so let's just dive right in. You have an incredible story. What has been one of the most challenging obstacles you've encountered?

Erica: I can actually come up with two significant obstacles. One was a previous marriage, during which I experienced severe physical and emotional abuse. I had three children with him, and towards the end of that marriage, we had moved to Mexico. I tried to leave him maybe eight or nine times, but I always ended up going back. Despite the abuse, that life felt comfortable to me. It was what I knew.

The turning point came one day when a neighbor of mine was visiting. She knew all the intimate details of what was happening, and she just put her hands on my shoulders and said, "Erica, if you don't get out, he's going to end up killing you." And I knew she was truly looking out for me. She was a real friend.

I really took her words to heart, and the realization that gave me the push to leave was when I asked myself, "If something serious happens to me, what would happen with my kids?" So I dug deep, found my courage, took the kids, and I left him. I actually fled the country, moved back to the U.S., and lived with my parents in Irvine, California. I went back to school, and that's when I really started using and trusting my intuition, my own gut instincts. I knew I needed to push forward in order to provide a better life for my children.

Kimberly: I think it's important to point out that when a woman is trapped in a domestic violence situation, on average, she'll go back about seven times before finally mustering the courage to leave. I'm glad you mentioned going back, because it's important for people to realize this is a process that takes time. It doesn't happen all at once. It takes a few tries to finally get out for good.

Erica: Yes. It was extremely scary, but when you're in that kind of situation, fight-or-flight kicks in, and you do whatever you have to do to get out.

Kimberly: And what was it that helped you overcome your fear of leaving?

Erica: I just knew this was what I needed to do for my kids. I mean, I was so broken, I had so little self-esteem, and I really feel as if there was some divine intervention. I just knew what I had to do, and why I had to do it.

After I moved in with my parents and found a safe place to recover, I really started understanding that I did have this strong spiritual connection. I did have intuition, and I took a lot of classes where I worked on developing my relationship with that divinity.

I started taking workshops run by a company called Intuitive Development. I met a whole community of like-minded people, and it really felt like I was being saved. I started realizing that maybe I did have some value. Maybe I did have something to offer others.

Kimberly: Absolutely. Realizing your own self-worth is powerful. Reaching out to different communities for help is also powerful.

Erica: Yes, and because I was so isolated in Mexico, once I found this new community, I realized how important human connection is. And you know, it's still very important to me to this day. I think, as a collective, we're starting to realize how important community is.

Kimberly: Yes, we are. So, you said you had two obstacles. What was your other one?

Erica: My other obstacle was when my adult daughter suffered a severe psychotic episode. It ended up being a two-and-a-half-year journey, and it was really her healing that created the need for me to go inward and do more work on myself. I feel like I had two spiritual awakenings in my life. One when I left my abusive relationship, and the other as a result of my daughter's trauma.

I sought out shamanic healing for her, and I began working on myself on a whole other level. I focused on energy and breath work, and as I became more self-aware, I realized I played an extremely crucial role in my daughter's mental and emotional health. Possibly the most crucial out of anyone.

A lot of her pain had to do with me, and as a parent, I had to own up to that fact. I didn't feel like a bad parent, not by any means; I was busy trying to pay bills, and I was mostly focusing on daily life's issues. I wasn't being emotionally available to her, or any of my other kids. So it was through this process of helping her recover that I found myself and started getting in touch with who I really was. When we were together, I was finally able to be fully present with her, and we created this absolutely magical space where we both had the opportunity to heal as mother and daughter.

Healing myself through her has benefitted every other relationship in my life. It benefitted my relationships with my other two children, my relationship with my husband, with my friends, everybody. The more I connected with that deeper, fearful part of myself, the more I could connect deeply with the people around me.

Kimberly: It really changes your perspective on everything, doesn't it?

Erica: Yes. When I took my daughter in for shamanic healing, the shaman said to me, "Are you doing your own work?" At the time, I didn't know what exactly he meant, but I remember thinking he was talking about negative beliefs and how I'm supposed to get rid of them or something. But I didn't know how.

As a child, my main coping mechanism was to completely shut down, and that strategy carried into adulthood. I put up such a huge barrier around my heart, just to protect it. I lived most of my life in a state of numbness. I had a nice life, great career, great friends, but I couldn't really appreciate all those blessings the way I can now.

Kimberly: As mothers, we often forget to check in on ourselves. We usually think we're secondary, that we're not as important as our children, but that's not true. We're just as important, and if we don't work on ourselves, then we can't really help guide our children.

Erica: Yes. My shaman, a wonderful woman named Cyndi Flagg, invited me to look within using various tools like meditation, energy work, and breath work. For me, the primary tool was Transformational Breath®, and the reason it was so important was because it allowed me access to myself.

When you're meditating, you quiet your mind and become present with yourself. Now, I wasn't the kind of person who could sit and meditate, because my mind would just keep going. That's why Transformational Breath® was the primary tool, because all you have to do is breathe in a certain way. I started noticing subconscious feelings and beliefs coming to the surface, and I learned to let go of the beliefs that no longer served me.

It's easier for me to meditate now, because I've been able to face my fears, and I feel like I've put a lot of work in. I am more at peace now, but at the time it wasn't, because of the emotional crisis I was in. I think back then, I was afraid of what I would find if I went inside.

Kimberly: We all are. Everybody has that same fear. Everybody is just as afraid to feel as you were.

Erica: Allowing myself to actually feel my feelings has helped me gain some compassion for myself. It's been a very warm experience, because I think I had been rejecting the frightened little girl in my heart, if you will, for so long. I didn't think I was lovable, so I internalized a lot of self-destructive feelings and attitudes. Now I can recognize that as the coping mechanism that it was.

Kimberly: Yes. Exactly. Now, I want to quickly go back to your podcast. It's called Twice Deleted, and I find that name really interesting. How did you come up with that name?

Erica: Well, I came up with after continuously asking the Spirit for a name. I couldn't think of a good name that was catchy, but also communicated the message behind the show. I just woke up one morning, and I had the name in my head: Twice Deleted. The name makes sense, because my daughter actually had two severe psychotic episodes, and I also had two severe traumatic experiences in life where I basically had to start over. So Twice Deleted made perfect sense.

Kimberly: I think it's a great name. So let me ask you, if you could give your younger self one piece of advice, what would it be?

Erica: Oh my goodness, I would tell my younger self not to be afraid of feeling her feelings. I would tell her not to dim her inner light, because she is extraordinary.

Kimberly: A lot of little girls don't know that. No one tells them. It all starts with people telling us how we're supposed to look, how we're supposed to dress, and we almost begin our lives feeling disappointed for not living up to what others think we should be. I think that's perfect advice, Erica.

Erica: Yes. Oh, and I would also like to add one more thing. I would remind my younger self that she is unconditionally loved. There's a huge source of unconditional love within her, and it's just waiting for her to see it.

Kimberly: That feels like a big hug. I love it.

Erica: I'm at a point in life where I can finally see all the little paths and bridges that led me to where I am today. It was a challenging journey, and there were so many moments when I felt things would never improve, but they did, and I feel absolutely blessed to have lived this journey.

Kimberly: I love it. Would you tapping into the breath was one of the tools that helped you the most?

Erica: Yes. There is no doubt about it.

Kimberly: It's magic. I don't think people truly realize the power of breath. That's why I wanted to come back and just touch on that again, because when you're able to tap into something we already do automatically, it literally transforms your life. It allows you to heal, it gives you courage, and it gives you strength.

Erica: Yes, absolutely. A great analogy my brother-in-law shared is that when we're children, we all start each of our lives with an empty wheelbarrow. Life happens, bad things happen to us, and over time, each of these painful events becomes a rock that is placed in the wheelbarrow. As we continue living, the wheelbarrow becomes heavier and harder to push. Every breath work session is like taking one little rock out of the wheelbarrow, and it's like you're lightening the load you've been carrying with you your whole life.

Kimberly: Powerful, powerful stuff. I have absolutely loved our conversation. Thank you so much for sharing your story with me. It's truly wonderful that you're able to sit in this space and share, because your message is very powerful.

Erica: Oh, thank you. It has been an honor to be a part of this. I truly appreciate you and everything you do.

CHAPTER 7

It's Perspective

Genevieve Espinosa

Genevieve has served in the Marines, she has been a military wife, she is currently a mother of five, a successful business owner, cosmetologist, a lifestyle coach, a world traveler, and an award-winning artist. In 2013, she received the highest honor a military spouse can achieve: the Dr. Mary Walker Award, thanks to her contributions improving the quality of life for over 30,000 military families and soldiers.

She is a giver with a big heart. She lives by the mantra "When you change the way you see the world; the opportunities are endless." That mantra was put to the test when a tumor was found in her daughter's brain. Over the past twelve years, her daughter has undergone multiple surgeries to remove the tumors, and she is currently fighting her third. Genevieve's positive, altruistic outlook was challenged during these times, but she still continues to shine, despite the tragedies that have befallen her and her loved ones.

Positivity and self-motivation are Genevieve's calling. She works to make the world a brighter, happier place, even in the midst of suffering. Today, Genevieve is pursuing her creative endeavors, living the life of her dreams in Arizona. She is married to her longtime husband, watching their children grow and build lives of their own.
gmespinosa75@gmail.com

"Looking through to the other side, she stayed positive and strong." ~K.A.

It's Perspective...Genevieve Espinosa

Kimberly: I am thrilled to introduce Genevieve Espinosa. Genevieve, you've done amazing things. You've helped 30,000 people, and you're receiving an award for it. Share more about that.

Genevieve: It was a lifetime achievement award. When I started volunteering, I didn't know you could be awarded for that kind of work. I began my volunteer work as a Marine Corps wife, then after going through a divorce, I stopped, and I was a single mother for five years. Then, after my current husband and I fell in love and got married, I started volunteering all over again. It was really about working with and supporting the spouses of deployed soldiers.

It's especially important when younger women are involved, because they're still growing and developing. I've been in their shoes, we all have, and I feel that we owe it to them as women, no matter what their circumstances might be, to share their stories and lift them up. Often, we feel intimidated, or we feel inferior if we seek our sister's help, but in fact, that's not true at all.

When you experience trauma or difficult moments, the thing that sets the people who overcome apart from the ones who don't, is perspective. It's the way that person interprets things. When people are put under pressure, some of them crumble, while others rise to the occasion. The people who rise to the occasion are usually the ones who put their hardships into perspective, and actively work to maintain a positive outlook.

For example, right now we're all stuck in our homes, and everyone feels isolated. We can't go out and do the things we want, and many of us feel cooped up. Feeling cooped up is a choice. Instead of feeling claustrophobic and tense, we can take this time to work on ourselves, to do projects around the house we always wanted to do but never got around to. We can spend quality time with the people we never used to have time for.

My husband is currently working from home. Normally, I wouldn't get to see him, but now he's here, and he'll come in the room and visit me. He'll give me a glass of water or something, you know, something to let me know he's thinking about me, and then he goes back to work. They might sound inconsequential, but it's nice to have those little moments with him. Instead of feeling sad that I can't get on a plane and visit our children, I have chosen to accept and savor the blessings I still have.

I believe after this pandemic is over, we're going to have a better understanding of the value of our lives, and we're going to cherish the things, and the people, that truly matter. Corona is our Great Depression; it's our world war. This is the moment our entire world shuts down, and we all have to stop, reflect, and change our perspectives. Right now, we're still in the thick of it, but I'm curious to see what we'll do and how we'll change once this is over.

Kimberly: I totally agree. I think it's interesting you brought that up, because perspective is everything, and Mother Earth is taking this pause right now. She's healing, and that also gives us a chance to heal, and gain a new perspective of how exactly we've been living our lives. And like you said, after this ends, how are we going to live our lives from that moment forward?

Genevieve: Right. And I think, in the long run, it will make us value our friendships a lot more.

Kimberly: Now, you've worn many hats, so to speak. You've done many things and you've traveled all over the place. But for now, let's talk about some of the obstacles you've overcome.

Your bio mentions your daughter, so, if you're okay with it, I'd like to start with her.

Genevieve: I think most parents don't expect anything bad to happen to their children. We're very protected now, and for the most part, children and babies don't have the high mortality rate they did in previous generations. It used to be that babies weren't given a name until they were about a year old, because there was always the possibility they wouldn't survive that long. Severe childhood illnesses are much less common now than they were in the past.

However, when my daughter was in sixth grade, she started having headaches and not feeling good. I knew she was sick, and I kept taking her to the doctor, thinking the doctor would tell us it was just a migraine or something. But after several trips and several appointments, we tried all kinds of different medications and nothing seemed to work. The doctors finally ordered a CAT scan. My daughter had a tumor in her brain the size of a plum.

She was admitted into the hospital, facing brain surgery. Now, if we had lived even twenty years ago, she would never have survived. But she did. She recovered, and she went on to do all kinds of great things. But two years later, it came back, and we had to face a second surgery.

At the time, my husband was serving in Afghanistan. He immediately came home on emergency leave. The doctors did the surgery, and two weeks later, my daughter was released from the hospital. My husband flew back to Afghanistan, and it was up to me to take my daughter to physical therapy, speech therapy, occupational therapy, and her art therapy appointments.

Despite these setbacks, I tried to focus on the positive aspects of my life, instead of dwelling on the negative. My husband was in Afghanistan, he wasn't there with us, but in a way he was. He gave us that home, he gave us love, he gave us everything we could've asked for. I was grateful for what I had, and that was my perspective.

That's the difference between a positive person and a negative person; a positive person still feels negative emotions, but they don't get trapped in them. They'll get back up and turn their painful situation into something positive, because they know things will get better in the end. And that's what I did. I trusted things to work out.

I'm glad I've been able to keep that perspective, even in the middle of challenges. I mean, I had a difficult childhood, then I got divorced. I was a single mother raising three children, I put myself through cosmetology school, and yeah, it was difficult. But I never dwelled in the negativity. That's what I tried to teach when I was a lifestyle coach. I tried to teach women how to shift the way they think, instead of feeling defeated by the situation.

Kimberly: She's going through her third round of treatment now, right?

Genevieve: She is. A third tumor appeared, and she's going through treatment. We're trying a new therapy called radial surgery, where they build this cage and put it on the front and back of your head. It's supposed to keep you from moving. They take a laser beam and literally spin you around slowly as the beam targets the tumor. They're trying to hit the tumor from all directions. It sounds pretty scary, but it's not as invasive as physical surgery, so there's no risk of an open wound becoming infected or something.

We've actually been very blessed that her tumors have not been malignant, just persistent. So the problem seems to be that there are just leftover cells, and the cells start dividing, and once they pick up speed, the tumor grows faster and faster. So it's still the same tumor. Technically. It's currently very small, so hopefully it will shrink and atrophy after it's been damaged. It'll take about twelve to eighteen months or so for the doctors to know if this treatment will be successful.

It was strange; we weren't allowed to go into the hospital with her, because of the virus, so we had to take her to the oncology appointment and sit in the parking lot while she received treatment. After the surgery, though, she walked out with the nurse. She wasn't using a wheelchair, she wasn't walking with crutches, a brace, or anything.

We took her home afterwards. She stayed with us for a few days because she was feeling tired, but then after a little while she wanted to go back to her own apartment and her own life. And that's a good thing. She's handling all this very well.

Kimberly: That's great to hear.

Genevieve: She has a good quality of life. She's an artist, she does her own thing. She's living her best life, and that's all any of us can do right now. No matter what the world throws at us, virus or otherwise, all we can really do is live as well as we can in each moment.

Kimberly: Do her tumors cause any other kinds of medical issues?

Genevieve: Yes, there are other issues, as you might expect, but that just comes along with having had multiple brain surgeries. It has affected the family, because there have been some personality changes. There have been mental health issues and things like that, but of respect for her privacy, I don't want to say too much about them.

Kimberly: Absolutely. Let's change it up a little. If you could give your younger self one piece of advice, what would it be?

Genevieve: I would definitely tell my younger self to not be afraid. I'd tell her not to underestimate her unlimited potential. I would have loved to have heard that as a young girl, but I didn't, so I had to learn that lesson the hard way. We have to go through those painful or traumatic experiences before we can learn some really important life lessons, but once we've survived those traumas, that's when we gain some wisdom.

Kimberly: Fantastic insight. So, I'm really happy to hear your daughter was only in your house for a couple days after the surgery. How awesome is it that she can literally have brain surgery, then say, "Mom, I want to go back to my own apartment?"

Genevieve: It was incredible. I'm so happy she was able to go back home so soon. She'd been giving me a hard time up until the day of the surgery, but I think she was just feeling fear. She was afraid of losing her independence, and so she pushed me away, rather than admit I could help her. And you can't really blame her; that's a scary thing to go through. But she's calmer now, and she's in a much better place, emotionally.

Kimberly: Absolutely. I just wanted to take the time to recognize her bravery. And your bravery too, for taking this on three different times.

Genevieve: I had to. And it was hard, because I've got a life of my own going in the middle of this chaos. All my kids have moved out of the house, so I'm an empty nester now, and this really is a new phase for me. They all have their own places and their own lives, so now I'm asking myself what is my new role in their lives? I love them, and I want to know what they're up to and how they're doing, but they don't need me as much. It's definitely a new experience for me.

Kimberly: It sounds like they're going through new phases, too.

Genevieve: They are. Everything changes. Nothing stays the same. Even if you don't physically try to change your life, life still changes around you, so you might as well go with the flow and become an active participant in your own journey. They're sheltering in place and keeping safe, so I'm happy about that. I'm keeping busy.

I'm currently not accepting any new coaching clients, because I've been doing some illustrating. You actually asked me to work on a project with you, so I've been illustrating, what, maybe forty-eight tarot cards?

Kimberly: Forty-four cards. And that's just one deck! We have more decks coming down the pipeline. I was just in awe over your artwork.

Genevieve: I'm excited about this desk, because I think it's going to be one of my favorite tarot decks. The female energy that went into making this is really going to come through. I'm super excited. I've been drawing and designing goddesses, and I would come up with what they needed, what they didn't need, and so on. I'd show them to you, you'd give me some feedback, and I would incorporate your feedback into the next design. It's been a true collaboration, I'm very excited about it, and I can't wait to share these cards with people.

Kimberly: It was an amazing collaboration. From picking the goddesses, doing the illustrations, and then intuiting them – it's been an incredible experience. It's a great deck, and I can't wait for you to share it with everyone. Thank you so much for sharing, and for everything you do.

CHAPTER 8

Do It With Fear

Jeimy Reyes

Jeimy Reyes (founder of Sisters Making 6 Figures) was born in the Dominican Republic. She moved to Puerto Rico when she was eight, and when she was a young woman, she moved to California. She is a wife and mother of two boys. For the past five years, she has empowered women to become better versions of themselves, culminating in the founding of Sisters Making 6 Figures.

Jeimy is an incredibly generous person who surrounds herself with powerful women. She is a social media and networking marketing mentor. Over the years, she has built a community where women collaborate with one another, working together for the purpose of generating wealth in their lives.

*"An entrepreneur at heart – from the very beginning;
her mission has been to empower others." ~K.A.*

Do It With Fear...Jeimy Reyes

Kimberly: I'm excited to introduce Jeimy Reyes. Jeimy, you have done so much in your life. Please share a little about yourself.

Jeimy: I was born in the Dominican Republic. I came from poverty. Growing up, I didn't have much. My family had no lights, so when we ate, we ate in the dark. At a young age, I learned the value of the simple things in life. I learned the value of being a generous person, sharing what you have with others less fortunate, even if you don't have much yourself. My family moved to Puerto Rico when I was sixteen, where my father introduced me to the network marketing space, and I've been working in that field for the past seventeen years.

My father taught me what it meant to be a business owner, what owning my own business would entail, and so on. As a young woman, I didn't really know what I was going to do with myself. My father wanted me to become an engineer like he, my sisters, and my brother were. I chose not to do that. Instead, I became an interior designer, like my mother.

I can't emphasize enough how much my father taught me. He was an entrepreneur and a loving father, and he showed my sister and I nothing but encouragement. Since he ran his own business, he really was my first mentor, and as I grew older, I followed in his footsteps. I already knew I didn't want to be a schoolteacher, but I did want to mentor people. When social media took off, I began teaching social media marketing. I taught companies how to advertise and market their businesses on social media, and as a result, I became fairly well-known online.

But I should go back and give you a little more background about myself. At age sixteen, I finished my career in interior design, then I explored other careers that really weren't for me. When I was twenty, I got married and had children, and I've been married for almost eleven years now. We are very happy to be young, married entrepreneurs. Motherhood can be very challenging, so I started using social media to teach mothers who feel overwhelmed. I know what they're going through. I know their struggles. I've been through many of those struggles myself.

In 2012, I moved from Puerto Rico to California. I didn't know English; I only knew Spanish. I learned English from watching Charmed on TV. A lot of people started asking how I spoke English so well, and my answer was really simple: I just know how to listen. I needed to listen and practice, and pretty soon, I landed my first job in the United States – I worked as a cashier at the 99 Cent store. A large part of that job would require interacting with customers, and I told the manager I didn't know English very well, but I was still a very hard worker.

At this time, I was still involved in the network marketing scene, but I wasn't going anywhere with it, due to my fear of speaking English. But I knew I had to get out of my comfort zone and overcome that fear. It's very important to get out of your comfort zone, which is what I did when I told my manager I didn't know much English. My manager was originally from Guatemala, so she understood what I was going through.

I just started speaking with everyone who came into the store. I lived in Temecula, and I pretty much got to know the whole town. It's not a small town, but if you work at the 99 Cents store, you're going to meet a lot of people. It was a good job, and I enjoyed meeting new people, but in my soul, I knew I didn't want to stay there. I knew I wanted to become my own boss.

Once, a woman came into the store and invited me to work with her cleaning houses. She told me I'd make more money with her. I was making eight dollars an hour at the 99-

cent store, and she told me I could make ten dollars an hour with her, so I agreed to work with her. We cleaned a few houses together, and then out of nowhere, she stopped calling me.

Now, I thought we were going to do more business together, so I'd already bought a new car. My husband and I had been making plans to send our son to daycare. Daycares were, and still are, expensive, and if you want to afford to send your child to daycare, you're going to need to work full time. I was still working at the 99-cent store, so I wasn't completely out of a job, but I knew I would need to start creating something for myself.

So I made some business cards for myself, and I started giving them out to people. I told my Zumba instructor that I had recently opened my own house cleaning company, and I just started promoting it.

Kimberly: You've done so many amazing things, but what I love most is that you don't let fear stop you. A lot of people really let fear talk them out of doing scary, and potentially exciting, things. You've shared interesting little tidbits about a lot of things, but let's go big. What would you say has been one of your biggest obstacles in your journey? Was it the language barrier, or was it something else?

Jeimy: Yeah, the fear of learning a new language was a big obstacle for me. I dropped out of a few of my companies because I didn't really know the language well. I just quit working with certain companies, because I was afraid no one would understand what I was saying. I quit the MLM company I was working for. I'm not working in an MLM company anymore, but at that time, I was. That's where I got my start.

So fear was a big obstacle for me, but eventually I realized that I had to leave my comfort zone. I couldn't let this fear cripple me. I decided to make that fear work for me, not against me. Now, when I mentor people, whatever they're afraid to do, I tell them to do it, and do it with fear. It's okay to feel afraid. We all feel afraid, but it's so important to continue working towards your goal in spite of that fear.

Kimberly: So powerful. I love that you're talking about this, because you lived so much of your early life in fear, yet you still kept pushing forward. So many people would've given in to their fears. So many people would have chosen to stay safe and hidden, but you didn't do that. I think that's incredible.

Jeimy: Yes. But it wasn't easy. It didn't just happen automatically. It was a process, and I'm grateful that I had several tools I could call on. I had to change my mindset, I had to work on personal development. I became a personal development junkie about five years ago.

I read The Cashflow Quadrant, by Robert. T. Kiyosaki. It was recommended to me by one of my coaches, who told me to read that before I started any kind of work on myself. I already loved reading, so that wasn't an issue, but I had never read a personal development book before that point. Once I started, though, my life changed, my world opened up, and I finally started tapping into my greatness. Once I started putting ideas from that book into practice, everything changed.

Kimberly: That's awesome. So, one of my favorite questions is up next, and since you became an entrepreneur at such a young age, you might have an interesting response. I was wondering, if you could give your younger self one piece of advice, what would it be?

Jeimy: "Don't waste your time. Listen." I could have accomplished so much more if I hadn't wasted time. I wish I could help people understand how important it is to not take any time for granted.

Kimberly: That's a very important piece of advice. And it's very true. You can never get time back. You can always earn money, you can replace material possessions, but you can't replace time. It's important you've learned that, and I think that is some extremely valuable insight.

Jeimy: Exactly. Time is a precious resource. I'm homeschooling my first-born right now. He's having trouble reading, so we're homeschooling him, and I'm enjoying every moment I spend with him, because I know I won't get those moments back once they're gone.

Kimberly: So true.

Jeimy: And honestly, I try not to live with any regrets. I try not to be too hard on myself for the time I wasted when I was young. I've done well now. I've created a community of female entrepreneurs who collaborate together, who empower each other, and who now have a vehicle for creating residual income. It's a community for women who want to become the best possible versions of themselves, but don't have the necessary tools to do that yet.

Kimberly: That sounds incredible. I love your wisdom, and I have totally appreciated our conversation today. Thank you for sharing with me, and thank you for telling your story. You've done so many amazing things, you've come so far, and I just love your point about not letting fear hold you back. Just power through it. Use the fear to your own advantage. The scarier an obstacle is, the stronger you'll feel after overcoming it.

CHAPTER 9

Stand Tall

Jennifer Gronbach

After struggling with depression, food addiction, and codependency, Jennifer found true help in the restorative power of her own breath. Through the Presence Process, meditation, grief work, and Transformational Breath®, she has healed physical pain, emotional wounds, she's cleared her mind of negative beliefs, and has begun to embrace her own authentic self.
As a result, she created the Breathing BEYOND Grief™ program to share her unique process of healing with others. Her mission is to help others heal from the inside out, so that they can truly begin to love themselves.

Transformational Breath® Senior Trainer and Grief Specialist
www.theclearingcenter.com
951-318-9833

"When she forgot who she was, she healed through breath work, and saved her own life, twice." ~K.A.

Stand Tall...Jennifer Gronbach

Kimberly: I am very excited to speak to Jennifer Gronbach. Jennifer, you've been through quite a journey, but before we get to that, I'd like to know a bit more about what you do.

Jennifer: I'm a senior trainer with the Transformational Breath Foundation, I'm a grief specialist, I own the The Clearing Center, and I'm the creator of the Breathing Beyond Grief™ program. Through integrative breath work, grief work, and tools for conscious presence, I can help you clear the clutter within, connect more fully with Spirit, and live life from a joyful place.

I love what I do because I get to empower people, and I get to share my own journey with others and pass on the life lessons I've learned, in the hopes that my experiences will help others. I love helping people clear all the emotional clutter they've gathered over the course of their lives. When my clients get rid of their negative beliefs and embrace who they are, embrace the divine spirit, and begin living their lives from a place of love – that's where I get my joy. From watching someone's positive transformation.

Kimberly: That's incredible. How did you discover the healing power of the breath?

Jennifer: In 2008 I suffered from severe depression, and I was suicidal. As a child, I was raised in a dysfunctional, alcoholic home, and I carried those scars throughout my life. I learned to survive by trying to be perfect, and staying out of the line of fire, but by 2008, at age 38, I just couldn't function anymore. I wanted to take my own life. I was in a really dark place.

I was introduced to integrative breath work through a book called The Presence Process. I read it, and that book was crucial in helping learn how to work with my breath, how to clear negative beliefs, etc. Once I started working with my breath, I was amazed at all the emotions that were coming out; repressed memories and feelings I had locked away, that kind of thing.

I was able to clear a lot of those feelings, and over time, I began working integrating concepts of present moment awareness into my breath work exercises. All these tools allowed me to reconnect with the truth of who I am, which gave me the courage to go into the depths of myself, where I had previously been afraid to go, and find my true self.

I realized I am beautiful, and I am powerful. I realized I was a divine being, a unique emanation of God. Because of my depression, I had forgotten who and what I truly was, and once I started realizing my own power, I knew I had to teach it. I had to share what I'd learned. I knew I needed to help people clear their own emotional clutter and experience the same transformational journey I had. That's when I started the Breathing Beyond program.

The program focuses on integrative breath work, the writing and communication process of grief work, and conscious presence exercises. It allows us to face our triggers so that we can be in charge of, rather than controlled by our emotions. We can learn to respond to our triggers in a way that empowers us.

Kimberly: I love that you talk about breath work, because breathing is something we do automatically, so it's not like you're learning a brand-new skill. You just have to learn how to focus on your breath. There's a lot of power in that.

Now, you mentioned depression. Has that been your biggest obstacle in life? Or if not, what would you say was your biggest obstacle to overcome?

Jennifer: My biggest obstacle was fighting for my life. I was fighting against my own sadness, my own negative thoughts and limiting beliefs. I was truly ready to take my life. I felt as if I would be doing my family a service. That really was the darkest period of my life.

In order to pull myself out of that darkness, I had to journey inward. I had to go into stillness, go into my own heart, and really dig deep to find that courage to stay alive. It was a real spiritual awakening. I reconnected with myself, and I reconnected with God, too. I wrote a song about the whole experience called "Stand Tall." It really helps me remember that I'm beautiful, and powerful. That song marked the beginning of my spiritual awakening, and it really pushed me to work on myself. It made me want to heal, and once I started, I cleared a lot of negative thoughts and attitudes I'd been carrying.

Fast forward to just a year and a half ago, when I was diagnosed with breast cancer. That was an interesting period in my life, because you'd think that would've been my greatest obstacle. And it was a huge obstacle, but it was easier to deal with because it felt more external than internal. It felt a little easier, because it wasn't me who wanted to take my life, it was the cancer. I had made so much progress, and I just decided I wasn't going to let this diagnosis throw me off course.

So I just kept using the tools I'd been using. I did my breath work, and so on. I had to strengthen myself, strengthen my immune system, and trust my gut. One of the most important lessons I've learned is to trust my gut. So it's been quite a journey so far, but I'm grateful for every obstacle in that journey, no matter how large or small. Some of the greatest gifts have come as a result of those challenges.

Kimberly: That's really interesting. I kept getting chills as you talked. That diagnosis wasn't that long ago, but looking at you now - you're just bringing this incredibly peaceful presence. It's coming through the camera.

Jennifer: I feel this overwhelming sense of calm, of connection. I'm very grateful for my journey, I'm grateful to be where I am today, and I'm so glad I have the opportunity to inspire people to remember who they truly are.

When you start the Breathing Beyond program, you're choosing to learn tools that will help connect you to your own spirit. Breath work is spirit work, and the more breath we bring in, the more spirit we're inviting into our bodies. As a result, we bring more divinity into ourselves. That's why breath work is the most important tool.

We have to connect with our breath. Through connecting with our breath, we are connecting with everyone and everything. Breath work helps us connect with the present moment. If we want to clear emotional clutter and free ourselves from the past's grip, the only way to do that is by connecting with the present. Dwelling on the past isn't going to get us anywhere, but becoming aware of the present is a life-saving tool. We'll never achieve true freedom unless we let go of the past.

Kimberly: I wanted to add that breath is prana. It's life. Once you realize that, it completely changes your perspective. It even gives you more energy!

Jennifer: Yes. 70% of our energy comes from oxygen, and many people don't realize the health benefits of taking a diaphragmatic breath. Detoxification is so important right now, especially since it helps lessen the toxins in our bodies. It gives us more energy, it helps with cellular regeneration, weight loss, and so much more. When we bring more oxygen into our bodies, we lessen our opportunity for disease. The more oxygen we draw into the body, the stronger our immune system becomes. Also, working with diaphragmatic breath stimulates our relaxation response. It calms our nervous system.

Kimberly: There are so many benefits in breath work. It's really incredible.

Jennifer: Yes. We can use our breath for oxygen, for energy, for emotional integration, for focus, for calming the mind, connection, for all kinds of things. We use it for everything. It's the greatest gift the Spirit has ever given us.

Kimberly: So, if you could give your younger self one piece of advice, what would that be?

Jennifer: "Always remember who you are." For many years, I forgot who I was. I was depressed, and I was disconnected from my true self. So I would tell my younger self to never forget the beauty, power, and divinity within herself. I would tell her to never forget who she is. My spiritual teacher used to tell me all the time: "Jen, you've just forgotten who you are." Then I would always get back on track. I would pick up my guitar, sing "Stand Tall" to myself, and that helped me remember myself. It's helped me so much.

The song reminds me that I don't have to be perfect. I don't need to have the perfect husband, the perfect children, the perfect job, a perfect house, or any of those things we think we need. The song is about how it's enough to just be who I am. The message is simple, but powerful.

Kimberly: You just gave me chills again.

Jennifer: I just want all the divine goddesses out there to know they are worthy. They are deserving of love, light, and joy. I want them to know it's okay to be who they are. We weren't put on this earth to be anyone else but ourselves, so just be yourself. Be who you are. It's okay.

Kimberly: I love that. We all tend to think we have to be all these different external things in order to be lovable, but at the end of the day, being who and what we are now in this moment is enough, and breath work will help you realize that.

Jennifer: Oh, absolutely. Just live life one breath at a time.

Kimberly: That's so awesome. I love what you do. I'm so glad you're sharing your journey with people, because you are really helping people transform, and it's amazing to see.

Jennifer: You're welcome. And thank you for having me.

CHAPTER 10

One Helluva Conversation

Kaprice Dal Cerro

After Kaprice earned her business degree, she knew she was meant to serve a larger purpose. She empowers businesswomen, identifying key business strategies that are tailored for long-term success. She's your business guide, carefully walking her clients through each step of the process. As a business mentor, her primary focus is you. As a busy wife and mother, she understands you're struggling to balance a business life and a home life. She understands that you need someone to help keep you accountable and help you move forward. Having Kaprice as your business mentor is like having a best friend helping you take your business to the next level.

Kaprice Dal Cerro
Business Mentor

Kaprice Marie, LLC
Kapricemarie.com

https://www.linkedin.com/in/kapricedalcerro
kaprice@kapricemarie.com
773-901-1059

"She holds your hand, compassionately leading you and your business towards the next level." ~K.A.

One Helluva Conversation...Kaprice Dal Cerro

Kimberly: I am so excited to introduce everyone to Kaprice Dal Cerro. She is an incredible woman. Please, Kaprice, share a little about what you do.

Kaprice: I'm a business mentor, and my approach is a little different from other coaches out there. My approach is very personal, and I'll often hold your hand, so to speak, through the process. I work very closely with my clients, I'm their cheerleader, and I explain business strategies in a different way that might make a little more sense.

Kimberly: You're right - a lot of coaches specifically tell people, "I'm not going to hold your hand. You've got to do this on your own." But there's also a whole group of people who actually need that hand-holding, so I think you're taking a really wonderful approach.

Kaprice: Thank you. That's what women kept telling me, when I was doing my market research. Some of them have taken so many business courses, but they're still lost. They tend not to finish the courses, because I think they finally reach a point where they're not sure how to push forward and integrate what they've learned into their businesses. That's when I come in. I give them that necessary push forward.

And I keep them accountable, too. I'm not going to slap my client's hand if she doesn't complete a certain task on time. It's more like I'm going to remind her she has a task to finish, and I'm going to try to motivate her and get her excited to complete it. I'm very compassionate, but when I work with my clients, we're working. We're not getting together for coffee. We're going to get serious about your business, but we're going to do it in a way that's comfortable and fun.

Kimberly: You're adding a little tenderness into the business world. I love that.

Kaprice: Thank you. I look at it like if someone's doing something for the first time and they're not sure what they're doing, it's okay to hold their hand while they do it.

Kimberly: Absolutely, especially in the world of entrepreneurship.

Kaprice: Absolutely. I just don't want my clients to feel lost. I want them to know I'm there for them.

Kimberly: So, let's start off with a big question. What would you say has been one of the biggest obstacles in your life, and how did you overcome it?

Kaprice: My biggest obstacle was overcoming my negative mindset, which is something I'm still working on. I was very, very afraid. I didn't think anyone would take me seriously, and not only that, but I couldn't think of a good reason why they should take me seriously. I think it stems from childhood, answering a question wrong in a classroom discussion, while your friends giggle and the teacher makes you feel inadequate.

I didn't feel very confident in myself. As a child, I didn't look the way young girls were "supposed" to look. I was an overweight child. My brothers picked on me, and I just didn't want people to look at me. I didn't want them to notice me, so I just didn't put myself out there.

And I became that quiet kid in the background, the one who has talents but doesn't share them, because those talents might make me a target. My toughest obstacle in life has been to let people see me for who I really am. Being vulnerable with people was not something I was good at, nor was it something I really wanted to be good at. My fears all stemmed from my desire as a child to not be seen.

Kimberly: Beliefs we develop as a child run deep, and they're difficult to get rid of. I can only imagine how badly you wanted to hide from everyone.

Kaprice: I didn't do very well on tests, so I would often feel as if I wasn't smart. I didn't necessarily get good grades all the time. That lack of confidence, all those fears really do travel with you as you get older. As an adult, you've developed your own set of crazy beliefs, and you just have to find a way to replace those negative beliefs with positive and uplifting ones.

Kimberly: If you think about what a belief is, it's just an idea that keeps getting reinforced. So if we don't get a good grade on a test, if we're overweight and we get made fun of, we feel we're not smart enough, or we feel that we're not attractive, and those beliefs all feed into that feeling of I'm not good enough.

We're constantly being bombarded with those negative thoughts, and we have to keep working on our mindset to challenge those thoughts. You're right; we have to keep replacing those unhealthy attitudes with positive ones.

Kaprice: Absolutely. It's why we need to be open to growth as well. We need to be willing to change who we are at our core. We need to learn it's okay to let our true selves show. But you're right, it's a constant struggle for everyone. In a world full of negative reinforcement, it's a constant struggle to be your authentic self.

Kimberly: What were some things you did to change your beliefs?

Kaprice: Well, I read a lot of mindset books. Those were very eye-opening experiences. I was just going inside myself and realizing I had a lot I wanted to accomplish. I knew I could reach my goals if I tried, but I just had to learn to believe in myself. Those mindset books helped me realize I wasn't alone, that I wasn't the only person in the world who felt these negative feelings. I got a lot of encouragement from that.

But, it's a continuous process. Even today, I have good days and bad days. I love reading, so I'm always reading new things. I'm always trying to keep my mind open.

Kimberly: A big part of that is just letting yourself have a bad day when you have one. It's just a matter of realizing even a bad day is part of the process, and accepting them as they come.

Kaprice: Exactly. If tomorrow I choose not to be productive, so I sit in my jammies and watch the Hallmark channel all day, that's alright. I must've really needed that break, so the fact that I took some time for myself is okay. Every so often, your body tells you that your mind needs to shut off for a little while, and there's nothing wrong with that.

Kimberly: There's that idea that we always have to be productive. I personally know some businesswomen who are also mothers, and they wake up at four in the morning so they can have an hour and a half to themselves before everyone else wakes up and the new day starts all over again. Now, that approach doesn't work for everyone, but it really comes down to finding out which approach works specifically for you.

Kaprice: Absolutely.

Kimberly: It's really empowering, once you start making decisions based on what's right for you, rather than say, what other people might want or expect from you.

Kaprice: It is. And you start feeling stronger, more confident in yourself. I used to be a huge people-pleaser, and guess what? I didn't feel confident about myself at all. But once I started doing things based on what would make me happy, my confidence went up, I was happier, and I started feeling proud of myself. I felt proud for finally standing up for myself. It's a powerful feeling, learning to do something for yourself.

Kimberly: This is a very important conversation to have. We need to empower women and teach them to do things for themselves, rather than just blindly saying "Yes" to the demands of others.

Kaprice: I one-hundred percent agree.

Kimberly: So, if you could go back and give your younger self one piece of advice, what would it be?

Kaprice: Oh, I have so much advice for my younger self. I would tell her to be herself. I would tell her to do what she wants to do, and don't feel scared about it. It took years for me to start challenging my own negative beliefs. It took years before I finally started trusting my gut and following my instincts. I would tell my younger self that it's okay for her to be the person she wants to be.

Kimberly: Can you imagine hearing that advice as a little girl? It would be so powerful.

Kaprice: Absolutely. It's like, why are we doing what we're doing? Are we doing it because we want to, or because someone else tells us that's what we're supposed to do? As women, are we getting married, having kids, doing all these things because we want them, or because that's what we're told a woman's place in society is? It makes you think.

I'm teaching my own children to do what makes them happy. I'm teaching them to follow their passions. If they don't want to work corporate, they don't have to; I won't push them into the corporate field. They should be able to pursue whatever life or career path they want, and if in ten years they realize that's not what they want, then do something else. Everyone grows. Everyone changes.

Kimberly: Exactly. That was a great little nugget right there.

Kaprice: Thank you.

Kimberly: I wanted to quickly touch on your podcast. Is it considered a podcast?

Kaprice: It's really not. I call it a video chat.

Kimberly: I love that. And I love the name of your show.

Kaprice: Thank you so much. It's called One Helluva Conversation: Real Women, Real Stories, and it's basically about women having conversations, sharing their stories, and talking about where they're at in life, how they got there, etc. I speak to women from all over the world, and what I've found is that even though we're all from different cultural backgrounds, we are all very much the same.

It's designed to empower, inspire, and inform. There's a lot of information in these videos about how women have helped themselves, how they've survived traumas and bad situations. It's really all about having an organic conversation and giving women a place to connect with one another.

Kimberly: I love the premise, and I love the name of your project. It reminds me a lot of why I started doing this series. It's all about connection. It's about sharing our own individual stories.

I have to tell you, Kaprice, this has been one helluva conversation. I wish we didn't have to wrap it up. I've absolutely loved chatting with you, though. Thank you for sharing your wisdom and your journey with us.

Kaprice: Thank you so much! It's been a pleasure.

CHAPTER 11

I Love Myself Enough To Do Something Different

Melanie Pederson

Melanie Pederson is a certified personal trainer, behavior change specialist, and she's the owner of a low carb/keto bakery. She is passionate about transforming lives in mind, body, and spirit. She helps people break free from negative mindsets and achieve the life they've been dreaming of. Melanie believes that with the right support, motivation, momentum, and knowledge, there's no limit to what a person can achieve.

She believes "innercise" needs to be done before nutrition and exercise can harness their full power and potential. After the birth of her second daughter, Melanie returned to college and earned a bachelor's degree in kinesiology with a minor in nutrition. She struggled to maintain a healthy weight during her adult life, and she spent years trying different nutritional strategies and exercise regimens. None worked for her.

After experiencing suicidal thoughts, she decided she was going to take her life back. She lost 103 pounds within the span of fifteen months, and made major changes to her mindset, her diet, and her exercise plan.

Melanie possesses the following degrees and certifications:
Certified Behavior Change Specialist – American Council on Exercise - 2018
Certified Mind Body Spirit Practitioner – Sunlight Alliance - 2015
Certified Health Coach – Institute for Integrative Nutrition - 2013
Certified Personal Trainer – American Council on Exercise – 2010
centerforlcl@gmail.com   https://www.facebook.com/centerforlcl

"She overcame obstacles and realized the importance of Innercise!" ~K.A.

I Love Myself Enough To Do Something Different...Melanie Pederson

Kimberly: I'm super excited to introduce Melanie Pederson. Melanie, you have a very profound story to share with everyone.

Melanie: Thank you for having me. Yes, I own the Center for Low Carb Living. I am a low carb/keto coach, a certified personal trainer, a certified health coach, certified behavior change specialist, and I run a low carb/keto bakery. I also offer online courses. I've got a bachelor's degree in kinesiology, with a minor in nutrition.

I educate, inspire, and motivate my clients to improve their quality of life. I attend seminars, I've completed several certification programs, and I've done a lot of healing. I finally reached the point where I realized I loved myself enough to do something different, which became my mantra throughout this journey.

In order to lose over one hundred pounds in fifteen months, I used every tool I'd learned. I went through a complete mental and physical transformation to get where I am today.

Kimberly: That's powerful.

Melanie: I'm very 'Type A,' and I'm an overachiever. Before I started improving my mind and body, I always knew what I needed to do. I knew exactly what I needed to change, but the motivation wasn't there because I didn't like myself. In fact, I hated myself. Honestly, I had gotten to the point where I was suicidal. I was experiencing suicidal thoughts, and that kind of snapped me back into reality. I realized I had the option either to take my life or take my life back. I was a mother, a wife, a sister, and a friend, and I realized how unfair taking my own life would have been to the people I loved.

I realized I needed to love myself. I knew I needed to do something different. Mind you, my self-talk was overwhelmingly negative. I was very abusive towards myself. I never told my husband any of the thoughts that were going through my head at that time, because if I did, it would've made him cry. It would have been too heartbreaking for him to know someone he loved was feeling such pain.

So I started fighting back. I started using tools I'd learned at all the retreats and clinics I'd gone to. I noticed I was gaining traction. I was seeing a real difference! Now, I don't want to say that losing weight is easy, because it's not. It's a chore, but it's also extremely rewarding. When I started cleaning up my negative thoughts, the fat started falling off. Yes, I was working out, I practiced good nutrition and all that, but changing my mindset really made the biggest difference.

Kimberly: Wow. That's absolutely incredible. I think we could talk for a week just about that.

Melanie: It's so important, and many people don't understand that.

Kimberly: I think that kind of leads into what your biggest obstacle was. From my perspective, it sounds like we've been covering it this whole time. Was your mindset the biggest obstacle you've had to overcome?

Melanie: My biggest obstacle was defeating my inner critic. I was harming not only myself, but others. When we feel ugly on the inside, that ugliness pours out onto everyone else, and I was so angry back then. I was vicious. I didn't even want to be around myself, so how could anyone else? I'm sure it was rough for my family.

In order to lose one hundred pounds in fifteen months, I really had to get a grip and defeat that nasty inner critic. I adopted the mantra "I love myself enough to do something different," and I repeated it constantly, even when it felt completely false. I had to keep repeating it until it eventually made sense.

And after working on myself for a while, I realized I did, and still do, love myself. I was finally able to look at myself in the mirror. For a while, I couldn't. I wouldn't even check to make sure my face looked okay. I couldn't handle seeing myself.

I started reading positive material like Louise Hay, Tony Robbins, Wayne Dyer, etc. I started learning their amazing stories. I started exercising regularly. I refused to let myself crash once more. I knew how rock bottom felt, and I didn't want to experience that again. I was constantly driven to change and improve. I worked on becoming healthy in my mind, because I knew if I could do that, my body would follow. I started practicing gratitude, and consciously reminded myself of all the little things I felt grateful for. And it really helped.

Kimberly: That's really important. Sitting in gratitude is great, because it instantly changes your perception and shifts your mindset.

Melanie: Fear, negativity, grief, sadness, guilt - all these things cannot coexist alongside gratitude and love, and for a long time, I lacked both gratitude and love. But once I started letting those positive feelings into my life, that negative critic hit the road. It was awesome.

Kimberly: You've spoken about the mental side of healing, but how did you transform and heal your body?

Melanie: I'm 5'11" and pretty tiny. At one point, I ballooned up to 253 pounds. I just started losing myself. I had gotten married, I started having children, and as many women do, I put myself on the back burner. I started packing on more and more physical weight. Every so often I'd lose a little bit of that weight, but not much, and those health practices never stuck. I was really grasping at straws when I eventually learned about keto. I was tired of wearing my husband's clothes, tired of crying at the store because I couldn't find any clothes that fit, so I started my keto journey. I started at about 232 pounds, and I got myself down to 129 pounds.

At that point, I felt I was getting a little too thin, and I didn't want to promote the idea that women need to be rail thin in order to be attractive. I wanted to promote health and wellness, so I hit the brakes right around 129, and now I feel great. I feel like I have freedom. I feel healthy in my mind, body, and soul.

Kimberly: That's incredible.

Melanie: I still had a lot of loose skin after that, which I didn't want, so I had an abdominoplasty to remove it. It's a pretty extreme procedure, but I went through it, and when I look back now, it seems like that procedure was my final goodbye to that unhealthy chapter of my life.

Kimberly: I love that word you used: "innercise." That's an awesome term. Often, we just think about exercise, but true healing doesn't only take place in the physical body. True healing happens in the mind and soul, too.

Melanie: It's huge. I've been a certified personal trainer since 2010, and I was thin back then. Then I gained a lot of weight, then I lost it. I've walked in both shoes. That's what makes me such a good coach, because I've been physically wrecked and unhealthy, and I've also been in good shape. I know how both of those experiences feel.

I've been shamed, made fun of because of my weight, I've been afraid to be seen in public. I can walk right alongside my clients, hold their hand, and they can trust that I'm not just reciting my lessons from a textbook. I'm speaking from my own firsthand experience. And, again, I know diet and exercise are important, but you're not going to see real progress until you start improving your mindset.

Kimberly: It's great that you've experienced both sides. You've been healthy and unhealthy. You can speak from your own experience. You've been there, done that.

Melanie: That's actually one of the things my husband tells me. Any time I'm struggling with an obstacle, he'll say, "You have go through this, because one day someone is going to come along and they're going to need to know how to get through it." When I'm struggling, that's usually not what I want to hear at all, but once I can sit and calm down, I realize he's totally right. I have knowledge and experience that someone is going to need someday.

Kimberly: Your husband is a wise man.

Melanie: He is. I'm very blessed to have him in my life.

Kimberly: I want to add something to this. I've experienced over twenty years in and out of domestic violence. I was so bitter about it, and I held onto that anger, because I felt like my life had been taken from me. But it was only through meditation that I realized I needed to have gone through that, in order to hold space for others who have experienced similar trauma. I needed to know how it felt, so I could help them.

Melanie: Exactly! Those experiences made us stronger, they've given us insight, and now it's up to us to serve the people who need guidance. And it doesn't happen automatically. Change and recovery don't just happen overnight. It's a slow, gradual process. You have to decide you want to do it. You have to make little adjustments each day, because your body can't just heal itself in a day. Early in my recovery, I would get angry because I would go on these 5k runs every day, but the next morning I wouldn't notice any difference in my appearance. The fat was still there, and I was so angry, I almost wanted to quit. But I had to learn that becoming healthy, in both body and mind, is a process that takes time.

Kimberly: Right. You have to make constant small adjustments in order to reach your end goal.

Melanie: I couldn't agree more. I mean, there were a few times I wanted to give up and quit trying to lose weight. When I started keto in 2017, it wasn't the big thing it is now. There were no special foods, no fancy trackers. If anything was low carb, it usually tasted like cardboard. In the beginning, I wasn't giving myself enough food, and I was hungry all the time. And when I'm hungry, I'm cranky, so I was really unhappy, and like I said, almost gave up.

I made little adjustments to my diet and exercise regimen. I started tweaking things here and there, until I finally found my sweet spot where I could eat healthy, yet still give my body the nourishment it needed. I started taking in enough calories where I would have the energy to exercise every day. Losing weight is not about starving yourself. You have to eat. If you're going to work out, or go for a run, your body needs proteins to function. It needs at least a little bit of those fats and carbohydrates in order to rebuild itself.

But every person is different, though. When my clients ask me to make them a meal plan, I don't. I'll tell them, in general, which foods are going to be healthy for them, but I'm not going to sit down and tell them exactly what they can and can't eat. They need to educate themselves. They need to take power into their own hands and learn about which foods work specifically for them.

Kimberly: I love that you're giving the power back to them. You're inspiring them to be proactive and make their own choices. A lot of people just show up and say, "Fix me, please," but you put the responsibility back into their hands. I love that.

Melanie: Yes. I've actually donned myself the "pint-sized pain in the ass," because that's kind of what my clients need. They need someone to push them just a little bit out of their comfort zone.

Kimberly: So, if you could go back and give your younger self one piece of advice, what would you say?

Melanie: Oh, man. Do you have, like, three years? There's a lot I would say to my younger self. But I guess the first thing that comes to mind is that I would tell myself I'm valuable. I would tell myself I'm worthy of love. And it's safe to love. It's safe to be loved. I would tell the younger me to prioritize herself, and not put up with toxic people; to set appropriate boundaries and appreciate the skin I'm in. I'd tell her it's safe to feel happy.

Kimberly: I love it. I love your energy, and I love your story. I'm excited to see how many lives you touch. Thank you so much for sharing your experiences. I think you're just amazing.

Melanie: Thank you so much.

CHAPTER 12

From Devastation To Joy, My Heart Showed Me The Way

Nancy Loeffler

Nancy Loeffler is the founder of Being with Grief. She is the author of The Alchemy of Grief: Your Journey to Wholeness, as well as its companion journal. As a mother who lost her 17-year-old daughter in a car accident, she fully understands the grieving process. Her daughter's death opened an unexpected doorway to Nancy's transformation. It broke open her heart, and showed her a way to free herself from limiting beliefs about what was possible in life.

She walks her clients through their own grief journeys, in the hopes that they too can find meaning, purpose, and even joy, after a devastating loss. She is passionate about changing the conversation around grief.

Being With Grief
Samyama Practitioner
Certified Eating Psychology Coach

www.beingwithgrief.com
919 500-3848

"Her journey is profound. Her healing work – transformational! From the rubble of tragedy, she excavated the heart-centered life she was always meant to live." ~K.A.

From Devastation To Joy, My Heart Showed Me The Way...Nancy Loeffler

Kimberly: I am so happy to introduce Nancy Loeffler. Nancy, your life has taken you on an incredible journey.

Nancy: Thank you, I'm thrilled to be here. And yes, it has. On November 3, 2000, my seventeen-year-old daughter Leah got into a car accident on her way to school. She was in the hospital for five days before she died. That was, by far, the most devastating and life-changing experience of my life.

When we left the hospital that last night, I had no idea how I was going to go on, or if I even wanted to go on. I had no idea what was next. I sleepwalked through the next few days, through the funeral and everything that went along with that. I wanted to stay in bed. I didn't want to feel all the horrendous feelings I felt.

About two weeks after she died, I received a message that said, "Losing Leah is too high a price to pay, to not live the life you were meant to live."

Kimberly: You just gave me chills.

Nancy: Yeah, I get chills every time I say it. I knew, in that moment, in order to honor my daughter, I needed to find a way to live that life. That's what my grief journey has been about, to excavate the life I was meant to live. That's what it felt I was doing, doing myself out of a deep hole.

That happened almost twenty years ago, and I've been creating that life for myself ever since. That's what led to my book, that's what led to me devoting myself to helping others navigate through their own grief.

Kimberly: I can't even imagine going through something like that. Do you have any other children, or was she your only?

Nancy: No, I have a son. He's thirty-nine. He was only twenty when she died, and it was a difficult time for him as well. My husband and I are still together. We found a way to make it through all that, which wasn't easy. We all worked through our grief in different ways.

I really couldn't help my husband or my son, or anyone else, for that matter. Leah's friends were coming over, and they wanted to connect, but I couldn't help any of them, because I hadn't met my own grief yet.

Kimberly: What did you do when you got that message? What was your next step?

Nancy: There was another message I received around the same time, which told me everything I had done up until that point had prepared me for what was coming next. I didn't know exactly what that meant, but I began a present moment awareness technique called Samyama. Samyama is from the yogic traditions, and it encourages us to sit with our feelings as they are, in each moment.

I knew I had to find a way to meet the feelings I didn't want to meet, and I called upon my practitioner when I needed someone to hold a space for me. She helped me begin to process my feelings, and allowed me to sit with those raw feelings as they were in each moment. In the early days of the practice, I would mentally revisit the moments before my daughter left for school and try to find a way to change the outcome. But as I turned myself over to Samyama, which is a heart-centered practice, I began learning how to sit with my feelings as they showed up.

Kimberly: That is a very, very difficult thing to do, but once you learn how to do it, it can profoundly change your life.

Nancy: It taught me to live in the unknown. We think we know everything and we think we can control things, but we can't. We are always living in the unknown, and as I began to realize that, I began to embrace the unknown. I embraced the feelings that came with not knowing, and I noticed my feelings beginning to shift. I wasn't ignoring them anymore, I was paying attention to what they were trying to tell me.

Often, when we feel something, we're associating a memory with the feeling, rather than just feeling the emotion. In each individual moment, our feelings change a little bit. What we're feeling in this moment might not be exactly the same as what we felt in the last moment, because now we're in this moment.

The more I focused on that, the more I started receiving blessings and grace, just from having the ability to hold onto my feelings as they came. When I noticed how profound this felt, I knew I was being called to become certified. I knew it was my mission to help others process their own grief.

Kimberly: That's amazing! Can you share a little more about that process? I don't think a lot of people know what Samyama is.

Nancy: There are three levels of Samyama. The first level involves learning how to bring awareness into our hearts. I grew up knowing I had a physical heart, but not a metaphorical heart. I didn't know how to "be in my heart." I would hear the term "heart-centered," and I had no idea what that meant. The first level of Samyama is about bringing awareness into our hearts, which is done simply. I teach my clients to become aware of their breath. And I have several different awareness exercises I could teach, depending on what a specific client's experience level is.

The second level of Samyama is the meditative aspect. That's where we begin to notice the edges are getting a little softer. We're able to be in our hearts and stay there for longer periods of time.

And finally, the third level is when our hearts, which are alchemical vessels, begin to shift our feelings. It's a feeling of alchemy, magic, or whatever you want to call it, but the feelings shift because they're held by the great heart, by the heart that is connected to us all. As we begin to shift, we get insights. Everyone I've worked with receives these insights, in one way or another.

That's a very short explanation, but that's the basic structure of the practice. There's so much more to it than what I've described, and when I work with my clients, we go much deeper, but that's the basic idea.

Kimberly: So the practice helps you learn to stay firmly grounded in the present moment?

Nancy: Always. And when you can do that, when you have that tool in your toolbox, you start to learn that joy and happiness come from within. It's a very profound practice. After losing Leah, it helped me find meaning, purpose, and joy. It helped me go back and heal childhood wounds I thought I'd already worked on.

Kimberly: When you learn a new modality, or you put yourself in new situations, it brings up issues you thought you'd already taken care of. It's like peeling that next layer and going even deeper. We're constantly learning, constantly growing, expanding, and becoming more aware. There's so much to learn, and the journey never really ends.

Nancy: Exactly. When you're looking into yourself, you can always go deeper. My parents are no longer alive, but when they were alive, I had a difficult relationship with them. By using this practice, I've healed my relationship with my parents. I'm so grateful I found it.

Kimberly: What you and your family went through is so heart-wrenching. I can't even come up with a word to truly explain that level of grief. I can't imagine all the emotions you must have gone through. Not just grief, but anger. Hate. Questioning everything. Asking why this happened.

For you to have found this clarity and propelled yourself forward is truly incredible. I'm so grateful to you for sharing with everyone.

Nancy: Thank you. I still feel those negative feelings you mentioned. Sometimes people think losing my daughter doesn't impact me, just because I'm able to speak calmly about it. But of course it impacts me every day. And it's why I continue doing what I'm doing, working with my clients, practicing Samyama, etc.

Kimberly: Absolutely. It doesn't matter who you are or how high you've climbed in a company, there's always something that will stop us and take our breath away. There's always something that's going to stop us in our tracks, and having the tools you've discovered helps us process all those conflicting emotions. It helps us deal with it, basically. It doesn't erase the trauma, it doesn't take away the pain, but it does help.

Nancy: I agree. There's no ultimate destination we're traveling towards. It's a continual journey. After I began seeing clients, I received the message to write my book. I resisted writing at first, because I wasn't an author. I resisted until I got to a point where it became harder to resist the calling than it would be to write. I didn't know anything would happen with the book, and after I wrote it, I was called to speak about it and share my story. So that's what I'm doing now. I'm sharing my experiences, encouraging people to go on their own personal journeys.

Kimberly: I have one last question. If you could go back and give your younger self one piece of advice, what would it be?

Nancy: Play more. I've been searching for more play in my life. Looking back, I was a very serious child, for a variety of reasons. Now that I've gone back and healed my wounds, I've lightened up a little. Leah always used to say, "Lighten up, Mom." So, yes, I would tell my younger self to play more.

Kimberly: I love that. Even as adults, we can use that advice. We don't laugh enough. We don't enjoy being adults. We're caught up in all our responsibilities. We're wrapped up in our own childhood issues, still trying to recover from everything that's behind us. As an adult, it's very important to know how to play, so play. Have fun.

CHAPTER 13

Divinely Created For Greatness

Pattie Godfrey Sadler

Founder and CEO of New Life Clarity Project, Pattie Sadler is a published author, speaker, and influencer with a passion for creating global change. She has a talent for inspiring others to find the big WHY in their lives. She's a first responder and a gifted trainer, and she assists business owners, sales teams, entrepreneurs, and authors. She is a talk show host, a director of public relations in the SOaR Foundation, as well as the President/CEO of New Life Clarity Publishing.

Pattie lives life with passion, and has proved that it is possible for people to create life-changing results for themselves. She offers consulting on a comprehensive level and helps others turn their visions into reality. She is a heart-centered entrepreneur, and she creates spaces for others to share their stories and be heard.

http://newlifeclarity.com/
https://hearttalks.pro/
https://ezwaynetworktv.com

"Her story is powerful, her message profound, and she is on a mission." ~K.A.

Divinely Created For Greatness...Pattie Sadler

Kimberly: Pattie Sadler, thank you for being a part of this series. Please share a little about yourself.

Pattie: I'm super excited to be here. This is such a great opportunity for women to come together and share their stories.

First of all, I just want to give you a little bit of background about myself, then we'll get into the professional stuff. I want you guys to think of a woman, just picture a woman. It could be any woman and she's sitting in a closet, hiding. She's hiding from the man in her life, because she's afraid he's going to abuse her. Imagine this man emotionally abusing her. Imagine him telling her she's stupid, ugly, that no one else would ever want them. Imagine this man putting his hands around her neck, trying to squeeze the life out of her. Imagine this girl wondering what in the world she did to deserve this.

My heart goes out to women who have suffered domestic abuse. For seventeen years, I was married to a man who beat me and constantly told me I was nothing. And I believed I could save this man. As a woman, when we're young, we believe we can save someone. We believe our love can fix someone, but that's not the truth. We have to love ourselves first. Your love can save only one person, and that's you.

If we don't love and nurture ourselves, if we can't realize our value, then we won't be able to contribute to the world. We've all been blessed with different talents, and if you don't love and take care of yourself, you won't be able to reach your full potential.

When I finally made the decision to leave my abuser, I found myself on a train with a one-way ticket to California. It's been almost twelve years since I left that relationship, and let me tell you, I've experienced nothing but blessings ever since I made that choice. But I had to take that leap of faith. I had to take control of my own life, and I had to realize that I deserved better.

If anyone is in an abusive relationship, your situation isn't going to change until you change it. Love yourself enough to pick up and leave. Believe that there are others out there who will love and accept you for who you are, and get out.

Kimberly: Absolutely. And there are tons of resources out there.

Pattie: Definitely. I used to run a house in Visalia, California called Transition to New Life. It was a transitional house for women coming from incarceration. These women had everything stacked against them, and very few made it through the program sponsored by their probation. If anyone wants to make a transition in their life, if they really want to change and improve, they should absolutely reach out to me. I have all kinds of resources and connections. So take the plunge. It's worth it.

Kimberly: Would you say that an abusive relationship has been one of your biggest obstacles? As a survivor of domestic violence for over twenty years, I could totally picture everything you were talking about.

Pattie: Oh yeah, definitely. By leaving that marriage, I saved my own life, and I saved my children's lives. I've been able to take control of my own life.

Kimberly: What was it that made you decide to leave?

Pattie: I finally decided I'd had enough. No one can tell you to leave. You only leave once you decide you've had enough. I had to want to do it.

Kimberly: Well, then let me ask you this - what kept you strong? What gave you the courage to keep going?

Pattie: During the seventeen years I was with him, I had a strong belief in God. I believed I had a divine purpose, but all these other things around me were holding me back. I knew I couldn't do this alone, so I reached out to my higher power, and my higher power definitely gave me the courage and strength to keep pushing forward.

Kimberly: Domestic violence is such a broad spectrum of violence, and sharing these stories is what keeps us strong. I know a lot of women whose strength came from their children. They're not just leaving the relationship for their own good, they're doing it for their children's sake.

Pattie: When I left, I didn't have custody of my kids. I didn't know if I was going to have the opportunity to be a mother. I didn't know if they would even want me in their lives. When I took that leap of faith and left the relationship, I only had myself. But along the way, miracles started happening, doors started opening, and I knew immediately I had made the right choice.

I didn't know if I would see any of my kids again, but as I said, God brings miracles into our lives, and He certainly did that for me. Now my daughter is a part of my life, and has been for nine years. It just goes to show that you never quite know what miracles are going to happen when you take that leap of faith and make a bold decision.

Kimberly: That's so amazing. So how did you become a publisher, then? How did you bridge that gap from leaving that abusive relationship, to where you are now? And what made you decide to go into publishing?

Pattie: It started about eleven years ago. I felt I had an important story to share, and my whole healing process has been to share my experiences. I thought if I shared my experiences, maybe I could help someone else out there. So I started writing, and I began a program with another author, a bestselling author, and she served as my mentor for about four years. We worked on my story together, and I got myself published. I started doing writer's retreats, I started talking to people about spreading their light and sharing their stories.

About five years ago, I moved back to Utah to take care of my dad. He was in hospice at the time, and he passed away almost four years ago. Then for the last three years, I've been taking care of my mother. She passed away last month at 93, but when she was still with us, I couldn't leave the house; I needed to make sure she was supervised at all times. I had to find a way to work from home.

But again, miracles happened, and the good Lord gave me the opportunity to become a publisher, so I took it. We've grown since then, and we're doing really well. We have the ability to reach forty million potential retailers, buyers, and clients. We can create bestselling statuses for our authors. So the business has been growing, and so has my passion for people sharing their stories.

Kimberly: I love that. There's so much power in helping someone else by sharing our stories. It helps to remind people they're not alone, and that we're all walking this earth together. So then let me ask, what exactly is NLCP?

Pattie: NLCP is New Life Clarity Project, and that's the mother hub of everything I do. New Life Clarity Project is based on the idea that no matter what business I started, it would be a project to serve others. New Life Clarity Publishing is one of the subsidiaries of the New Life Clarity Project. Another one I have is Heart Talks, which is my speaking platform. I also have the Pattie Sadler Show as well.

Kimberly: Ultimately, you're creating multiple platforms for people to share their stories.

Pattie: Yes. I truly believe we are all divinely created for greatness, and that's even the slogan of New Life Clarity Publishing. Every single person on this earth has a story to tell. Every person's story has the potential to make an impact on you, and on the world as a whole. Everyone has a story that could potentially save someone else's life. That's why I started this company, and that's why I continue to do everything I'm doing.

Kimberly: That's so powerful. Sharing really is where the healing comes from. Now, if you could give your younger self one piece of advice, what would you tell her?

Pattie: That's a good question. There are so many things I would tell my younger self, but the most important thing would be to remind my younger self that I'm a daughter of God, divinely created for greatness. People have their own ideas about what their specific higher power is, but for me, it's God. And if we just remember we are created from that divinity, that the possibilities are endless, then we really have the ability to accomplish anything we want.

Kimberly: We have that power within us. It's the intuitive wisdom, the strength, courage, etc. They're all within us, but sometimes we forget. I think that's a powerful message, and I absolutely adore you. Would you like to impart any more wisdom before we wrap things up? I think the work you're doing is really profound, and it offers people such amazing opportunities to share their stories.

Pattie: There are a lot of things in the works right now. Things are still building and gaining momentum. The last thing I would say is that if anyone out there has a story they want to share, reach out to me on my website, www.newlifeclarity.com. Let me know you're interested in sharing your story, whether you want to be a published author, or whether you want to be on Heart Talks. If you want to make a positive impact on the world, then please get more information on my website. Send me a message. Let me know what you're interested in creating, because I'm interested in working with you.

Kimberly: Thank you so much for taking the time to speak with me today. I totally appreciate you.

Pattie: It's been an honor to be here, Kimberly. Thank you.

CHAPTER 14

Pushing Through

Ro Brown

Rolesha Brown owns and operates Sukari Spirits, a company dedicated to producing unique, handcrafted spirits. Sukari Spirits cuts no corners when it comes to developing and innovating its own brand of all-natural, ready-to-drink vodka spirit for health-conscious consumers. Sukari is vegan-friendly, kosher, gluten free, and GMO-free with no preservatives.

Rolesha Brown is the founder and CEO of Sukari Spirits, and a single mother to three wonderful children aged 22, 15, and 3. Before venturing into the spirits industry, Rolesha proudly served in the United States Air Force for eight years. After that, she served in the Air Force Reserves for an additional three years. She earned a BA in business and management from the University of Phoenix, and a degree in criminal justice from the Community College of the Air Force, as well as certifications from Bryan University in eDiscovery Project Management. She holds Lean Six Sigma certifications from Villanova University. She also enjoys spending time with her kids, traveling, running her business, as well as participating in outdoor sports.
rbrown@sukarispirits.com
https://www.facebook.com/sukarispirits
http://www.sukarispirits.com

"She persevered, no matter what life threw at her, before finally finding her way." ~K.A.

Pushing Through...Ro Brown

Kimberly: I am super excited to introduce Ro Brown. Ro, you make an amazing vodka spirit, so tell us about your business.

Ro: Sukari Spirits originally started as a brand of vodka made specifically for women. It's sweet, fruit-flavored, and a lot of women tend to like the fruit-flavored drinks. But when I started meeting more people, I learned that men were trying it, too, and they liked it just as much as women. The flavor's not overpowering, it's not overly sweet, and it's not very strong. Our vodka doesn't have that same burn other vodkas have.

It's made out of fruits and vegetables high in antioxidants. There's no hangover; it's vegan-friendly, it's kosher, and like all vodkas, it's gluten free. It's also non-GMO, but I was told we couldn't put that on the bottle.

Kimberly: It's delicious.

Ro: Thank you.

Kimberly: Why did you start making vodka?

Ro: Originally, I had a business partner who wanted to run a gym together. He wanted to P90X all day; I didn't. I couldn't. I couldn't do the hardcore workouts he wanted, and if I can't do the whole workout, how am I supposed to convince other people to do it?

We eventually decided to start an alcohol brand, because in my eyes, if you're going to start a business, it should be a business with sustainability. One thing you can guarantee is that people are always going to drink, shop, and gamble. As far as the gambling business is concerned, the casino industry was already monopolized. And retail's hard, because even though people are still going to shop during a recession, you still have to worry about getting product from your suppliers. When there's a recession, you have to worry about other variables, as far as going out of business and vendors no longer being available, etc.

So then only alcohol is left. For centuries, there have always been people who have made their own alcohol. It's always been around; it's always been a go-to for many people. We settled on starting our own alcohol brand, but my partner wanted to make tequila. I wanted to make vodka because it's one of the healthier alcoholic beverages. It can be mixed into just about anything while still retaining its original flavor.

Kimberly: And more people are more likely to drink vodka versus tequila. Plus, there are those of us adults who go, "Tequila? Nope! Too many bad memories."

Ro: Another thing about tequila is that it's very expensive to produce, unless you have family in Mexico with an agave farm. Also, because of an agreement the US has with Mexico, you can't use the word "tequila."

So we decided to make vodka, and after a few years, my original partner decided being in this industry wasn't something he wanted. But by this point, I had grown to love it even more than I thought I would. It was a business venture that I actually fell in love with, and years later, here I am - still doing it.

We also have sparkling pear Rose` that will hopefully be coming out soon; I'm waiting on federal approval. Then we're offering a honey peach whiskey sour. After I relocated to Georgia, I knew I had to create a flavor that represented the Peach State. Thus, the honey peach whiskey sour was born. Even though it's a whiskey, I kept women in mind while making it. It's a very smooth whiskey. We're sourcing both the honey and the peaches out of Georgia.

Kimberly: That's so exciting. I love that you're still in love with it after doing it all these years. How did you come up with the name?

Ro: I actually have to give my former partner credit for coming up with the name Sukari Spirits. I have to give credit where credit is due. Sukari actually means 'sugar' in Swahili, and I made a few changes to the design of the logo. Everyone used to say the S in our design looks like peacock feathers, so I changed it to resemble a phoenix's feathers, which in most cultures symbolizes strength and renewal. And that is a very good description of women – we're strong, we endure, and we always overcome.

Kimberly: Ooh, I like that. That's powerful.

Ro: When you look at the actual bottle, the shape represents women. The fullness and curve of the bottle represents a woman's curves. The etched gold text on the bottle's surface represents a woman's regalness and elegance. Basically, everything about the bottle's design represents women. We endure, and we persevere.

Kimberly: Yes we do, and I love that the bottle is sexy, the logo is sexy, the name is sexy and classy. It's an amazing design. And what I'd also like people to know is that you can just drink it right out of the bottle.

Ro: Vodka is versatile. Sukari is versatile, too. Like I said, you can mix it with just about anything – citrus sodas, lemonade, bad champagne someone gave you as a holiday gift, etc. You can have it on the rocks, or you can drink it straight. There are so many different options. Except dairy. I would not recommend mixing our vodka with dairy.

My favorite cocktail would probably be Sukari mixed with a little bit of coconut and pineapple. It's kind of a tropical drink. You can use Coconut Malibu rum and Pineapple Malibu rum, then shake, pour it over a little ice, and add a wedge of lime. It's delicious!

Kimberly: It sounds tasty.

Ro: It is. I've made frozen drinks at different events. The drinks I make depend on what the event is and what I'm doing there. I've actually made a frozen drink where I use coconut cream, like a strawberry daiquiri. I had a blender, added some Sukari, coconut cream, fresh pineapples, then poured it into a margarita glass and garnished it with a wedge of lemon. I brought a little bit of everything – lime, lemon, pineapple, even a little bit of mango. I'm always looking to see how versatile Sukari really is, so I make different cocktails for different events.

If I do multiple events in the same month and I know many attendees from the previous events will be there, I won't make the same cocktails. I want them to taste the versatility for themselves. Every time I create a new cocktail, I always post it on our website. I also started creating Sukari gummies.

Kimberly: Ooh, that's cool!

Ro: When most people make alcoholic gummies, they usually just buy the gummies, soak them in the alcohol, then spoon them out. I actually make my own gummies, and they're just like the ones you can buy at the grocery store. Just alcoholic.

Kimberly: I really like that you're creating alcohol specifically with women in mind. That's powerful, because when we think about a company that brews its own beverage, we don't usually imagine a woman running it. So to create an entire product with the female in mind – from the flavors to the company logo to the design of the bottle itself – that's just amazing.

Ro: Women are making strides in the liquor industry. There are so many different female-owned brands, from vodka to whiskey to wine, cognac, and brandy. Men might have started this industry, but women are pushing it forward.

Kimberly: You're creating an entirely new generation of people who can now drink and enjoy many types of cocktails specifically designed for them.

Ro: Exactly! You don't have to go out to a bar or club. Sukari is a ready-to-drink cocktail, meaning you can drink it straight or add a little something to it. It's really up to the customer.

Kimberly: I love it. I love that you're doing this. What has been one of your biggest obstacles in creating your vision, though? It could be a professional obstacle, or it could be a personal obstacle. Either way.

Ro: Oh, there have been a few hurdles throughout this journey. Losing a business partner was one. Having a daughter and going through the different open-heart surgeries she had, while still trying to run a business. I've had a lot of obstacles.

The main thing that's kept me going, though, is my three-year-old daughter. Even when I wanted to quit, all I had to do was step back and take a look at everything she's been through. She's had two open-heart surgeries, plus a few others, adding up to a total of five surgeries. And she's only three. She wakes up every day with a smile on her face.

So when I see her, I'm reminded there's nothing I can't make it through. If she can wake up every day with a smile, so can I. She's my power, and she's my strength. She is everything. If she can go through all that and still find the energy to smile, I have no excuse.

Kimberly: I want to go back for a second. When did you lose your business partner?

Ro: Late 2015.

Kimberly: So your daughter wasn't born yet?

Ro: No. As a matter of fact, I took over as sole owner of Sukari in February 2016, and I had my daughter in December.

Kimberly: Wow. So you were going through all that while pregnant.

Ro: Yes. You know that saying "What doesn't kill you makes you stronger?" That's definitely true in my case.

I was forty-two when I found out I was pregnant. I already had two other kids, and I was starting to ask myself questions. I asked myself, what do I have to show for my adult life, other than being in the military? Yes, I was about to be a mother of three, but what did I have to leave to them other than my life insurance policies? I wanted to leave a legacy. I wanted to show my children that all my hard work wasn't in vain.

I applied for business loans and was denied every time. Half the time they never even sent me a letter explaining why I was being denied. The other times, they told me I didn't have enough established credit, which was ridiculous. I had maintained a 720+ credit score! But that didn't matter to them. Unless you have an investor on your side, it's very, very hard to start your own business.

Kimberly: So it's like there's been this series of small obstacles that have happened, and it seems like each of these small obstacles just becomes fuel for your fire.

Ro: Yes. Exactly. Quitting was never an option for me. I needed to set a good example for my kids. I couldn't spend their whole lives telling them, "You have to finish what you start," then turn around and quit my business. I have to show them they need to work hard for what they want in life.

Kimberly: You just have to continue placing one foot in front of the other.

Ro: Exactly right.

Kimberly: So, I have one more question. If you could give your younger self one piece of advice, what would it be?

Ro: "Don't be so stubborn. Allow people to help you. I know you're used to doing everything yourself because that feels easier and safer, but sometimes you have to let other people help you. You can't do everything yourself."

Kimberly: So true. So powerful.

Ro: I can be stubborn and strong-minded. I'm used to doing everything myself, and it takes a lot for me to step back and allow other people to help me. My current partner has to remind me to let him help me sometimes, because I often try to take on all the responsibilities myself.

I've been this way for 40+ years, so it's hard for me to let someone step in and control an aspect of my life or my business. But I'm learning that you can't do everything on your own, especially in the business world.

Kimberly: But when you step back a little, what you're doing is allowing someone else to step in and share those successes with you. You're allowing him to feel empowered, which also empowers you because you're both tapping into your brilliance.

Ro: Exactly. I know my strengths and weaknesses, and one of the reasons I brought him in was because I knew I couldn't do all this myself. I would sometimes take meetings with people who didn't want to deal with a woman. They would rather make deals with a man, so when we'd show up to the meetings, the other parties would be like "Oh, so he's the brains and she's the beauty."

But once the meeting started and they started asking specific questions, that's when my partner would tell them, "Okay, you need to address that to her, because she's the brains and the beauty behind this business." There are some companies who will look at female-owned businesses and refuse to go any farther than that initial meeting.

Kimberly: Well, I'm so proud of you. I'm so excited for both you and your company. And thank you so much for your service. I'm grateful to you for being with me today.

Ro: Thank you so much for having me.

CHAPTER 15

It's In The Showing Up And Asking

Robbie Motter

Robbie Motter is the founder of GSFE (Global Society for Female Entrepreneurs). For over 28 years, she has served as the global coordinator for NAFE (National Association for Female Executives). She started 12 NAFE networks in California, four of which she runs herself.

In 2017, she founded a nonprofit that went on to become a 501c3 organization. Her vision is to create an environment where there are no barriers to a woman's success. Her mission is to empower women, inspire them, and help them become successful entrepreneurs. Robbie spent twenty-five years working in corporate America before becoming an entrepreneur. She is a marketing/PR consultant, a certified national speaker and author. She encourages women to SHOW UP, and speaks about the power of asking. In her words: "Women like to help, but they hate to ask."

She is a mother of three and grandmother to four. For many years, she was a single mother. She is currently divorced and lives in Southern California. Her goal is to inspire women of all ages, races, and backgrounds to succeed.
rmotter@aol.com
https://www.globalsocietyforfemaleentrepreneurs.org/
www.robbiemotter.com
https://www.facebook.com/robbie.motter

"This 'Queen Diva' devoted her life to helping as many people as possible. Thanks to her motto, 'SHOW UP and ASK,' she has changed countless lives." ~K.A.

It's In The Showing Up And Asking...Robbie Motter

Kimberly: I am super excited to introduce Robbie Motter. She is an incredible woman, and has touched the lives of so, so many.

Robbie: I'm honored to be on your show. It's just wonderful, because you absolutely do exactly what I do. You help women soar to greatness, and you know, that's something we need to do more of. There are so many women out there who feel completely alone. They need people like us they can call. That's where I think the "Ask" in my motto comes from. It's tough for women to ask.

Kimberly: That is so true. So, at what point did you decide you wanted to become an entrepreneur?

Robbie: When I was working in the corporate world, I had eight hundred people reporting to me. I was working in Washington, D.C. at the time, doing contracting work for the government. Before that, I worked in New York City. Anyway, I was climbing the corporate ladder, and I noticed that women weren't helping other women succeed. This was back in the late sixties. There was this attitude that helping or instructing women was a waste of time, that we didn't have what it took to succeed in business. I eventually decided I wanted to go into business for myself.

Anyhow, the last job I had in Washington, D.C., and I was able to turn that experience into being an entrepreneur. I started helping small businesses get government contracts, as I had acquired great knowledge in that field.

Kimberly: That's incredible. Now, what would you say has been one of the biggest obstacles you've faced, and how did you overcome it?

Robbie: Well, I used to be a very shy girl. Growing up, my mother was very disinterested in raising me. For the most part, I grew up in a series of foster homes. In 1985, my mother got sick. At the time, she was living in Northern California with her fifth husband. As her daughter, I felt I needed to quit my job and come out to California to help my stepfather take care of her.

I made the decision very quickly, and I packed up and moved out to California. Looking back, it was a good decision; that was the first time in my life I ever had any kind of relationship with my mother.

Anyway, I probably spent less than two years of my life living with my mother. I never knew my father, I never had any brothers or sisters, so I never really had any role models. When I was fourteen, I left one of my foster homes and took a bus to San Francisco. Once I was there, I interviewed with a company called Levi Strauss. I had no real experience, but I looked older than I was, and they hired me. Once I was hired, I showed up to work early, every day, just so I could learn everything I could about the office. And that was the beginning of my business career. After I got that job, I was never not working. Every job taught me something that would help me land my next job. I would meet someone who had heard about me, and that person would offer me a job with them. Every job was bigger and better than the last. I never even had to fill out an application! It was incredible.

Despite my success, I always felt I wasn't good enough. I didn't have a college degree. I never even received a high school diploma until I was in my forties, but I worked hard, and I was always lucky enough to land great jobs with great pay and excellent benefits.

When I was twenty-one, I moved back to Hawaii, where I was born, and I got a job at the Hawaiian Village Hotel. At the time, it was owned by Henry J. Kaiser and managed by Western

Hotels. I watched Mr. Kaiser lead his staff, and it was really incredible. He never took no for an answer. Once, I was caught in the elevator with him and a team of engineers. He wanted his engineers to build a round dome for the premiere of Around the World in 80 Days, and I heard them telling him there was no way to build a round dome. He kept shouting, "I don't pay you to tell me you cannot do it! I pay you to find a way!"

Then he turned to me and said, "Robbie, let this be a lesson to you - there is no such thing as a thing that can't be done. There is always a way." As I progressed throughout my career, I always kept that piece of advice in mind.

Kimberly: What an incredible life you've had. So, would you say your biggest obstacle was that you were shy?

Robbie: Yes. Very shy. It took a lot of work to change, but I eventually learned to take chances. I learned to step out of my comfort zone. So that's what I started doing. If you're taking chances, if you're constantly stepping out of your comfort zone, you can take bigger steps forward.

Kimberly: Where do you think that shyness came from? Do you think it might've come from being raised in foster homes?

Robbie: I don't know. I couldn't really say. I believe a person's past has nothing to do with their future. I believe your success - or your failure - is determined by what you do in this moment.

Kimberly: I'm curious about all the women you've had an impact on. Can you talk a little about your motto, "Show up and ask?"

Robbie: Well, you know, it's about showing up. Businesspeople have to show up. They need to be ready to do their job. And they have to make plans. They need to ask questions. They need to ask themselves, "What am I trying to achieve? Who are my customers? Where can I find potential customers?" If you're trying to increase your business, you want to be in places you're going to meet like-minded people. You need to ask potential customers or partners who they are, what they do, and what they need. You could go to five different events a week, and each one of those events might have different people who can open different doors for you. You never know who you're going to meet out there.

Kimberly: And, since we've known each other for a while, I know you have a personal story that really drives your "Show up and ask" philosophy home. Could you tell that story?

Robbie: As you know, I'm always telling people to show up and ask. Eleven years ago, I was at a meeting and someone said to me, "Well, you've never asked for anything you wanted."

So I said, "Okay. I would like a white, female Maltese dog. I want her spayed. No more than two years old." I love Maltese dogs, and two days later, one of my team members called me and said, "You don't know this, but I have that dog. I'm going through a divorce, and this dog is yours if you want her." The dog's name was Majesty, and I was affectionately known as the "Queen Diva." And I still have Majesty today.

Kimberly: That's awesome. I love how that story just proves the truth in your philosophy.

Robbie: The interesting thing is, I actually ask for stuff all the time. Just not for me. If someone tells me they need something, I'm out there asking for them. I'm trying to find someone to connect them with. Or if I meet someone I think needs to meet someone else, then I'll immediately connect them. I'm always searching out opportunities for my team members. I find opportunities, I share them with my team, but that's as much as I can do. If people don't want to take action, I can't make them take action.

Kimberly: It really is all about the asking and showing up, isn't it?

Robbie: It is.

Kimberly: So, if you could give your younger self one piece of advice, what would it be?

Robbie: "Don't doubt yourself. You're capable of achieving whatever you want." In the beginning, most of my jobs were in the payroll department. That's where I felt I needed to be – just working in the back office. When I got to the Hawaiian Village

Hotel, however, I started as head of payroll, but then I became their first director (which is now called Human Resources). Before long, I discovered my greatest skill is working with people, so I wasted a lot of time working in back offices. If I had confidence in myself, I could have progressed so much faster, but these days I know nothing is impossible. If someone really has the passion and drive to do something, they can achieve it.

I think women need to start taking a look at what they do and thinking about how they want to be remembered. In my case, I want to be remembered as the person who helped people make their dreams come true. I thank God every day for allowing me to do the beautiful work I do. I feel very blessed.

Kimberly: Absolutely. What would you say to someone who is trying to tap into their confidence?

Robbie: I tell my team members to make a list of everything of everything they've ever accomplished. Say you're a housewife, right? Well, you need to learn how to apply wallpaper, remove wallpaper, paint, etc. You weren't born with those skills, but you learned them.

And once my team started doing that, it really helped boost their confidence levels. One of my members recently told me she made her own list and was amazed at everything she'd accomplished. Sometimes it's important to give yourself a moment to pat yourself for everything you've done. It's important to give ourselves credit for our successes and accomplishments.

I've done a lot of things, I've accomplished a lot of things in my life, and I'm always looking to do more. I'm always pushing myself to get out of my comfort zone and accomplish the next thing. It could be little, or it could be something big.

Keeping a gratitude journal is very important. Every day, write down something you're grateful for. Even if you have a rough day, write down a list of good things that happened, or a list of things you're grateful for. Even if it's something as commonplace as sitting down at the dinner table with your family. Everything counts.

Kimberly: Such incredible wisdom, Robbie. These are all great ways to help people bring a little more confidence and gratitude into their lives.

Robbie: Yeah. I'll hear women come into the workforce and say "Well, I don't have any experience." Nonsense. They have plenty of experience – they've raised children, they've been house engineers, homemakers, they learned to cook, they learned how to make a schedule, how to fit household tasks in between raising their kids. They've learned so much, and they have so many skills under their belts. They just don't realize it.

Kimberly: Robbie, you are an absolute wealth of knowledge. Thank you so much for sharing with me today. This has been an incredible conversation.

Robbie: Thank you.

CHAPTER 16

If He Brings Me To It, He'll Bring Me Through It

Tameka Peoples

Tameka creates business plans and executable models of operations for public and private sector entities. She is an Air Force veteran, a small business owner, nonprofit founder, and a fearless leader. She is a Facebook "Vets-In-tech" winner, an LUSD Mentor of the Year, and recently, she has been awarded a multi-year, quarter-million-dollar grant by the USDA. This grant will go towards helping socially disadvantaged and veteran farmers. She has professionally managed and grown her firms to $19M+ in annual revenue, leading in the government space/IT sector. A visionary and leader in her community, she continues to create strategic partnerships with national organizations, while using her foundation to help people of color enter the tech field.

Peoples Foundation Non-profit | ABF – Consultant Firm | Apparel Production – Div. of ABF

Tameka R. Peoples
Founder/Board President

www.linkedin.com/in/tameka-peoples
Email1: tpeoples@peoples-foundation.org
Email2: tpeoples@abfcounsultants.com Email3: tpeoples@seed2shirt.com
O: 805.736.2959

"She is gracious and genuine, calm and fierce, and she has a message to share." ~K.A.

If He Brings Me To It, He'll Bring Me Through It...Tameka Peoples

Kimberly: I am thrilled to be speaking with Tamika Peoples. Please share a little about who you are.

Tameka: Thank you so much for having me. I'm so happy to be in this amazing space, having this conversation with you. I'm a small business owner; I own ABF Precision Consultants, and we do a lot of strategic planning for government clients, as well as larger primes that are in that space.

I also founded a nonprofit, the Peoples Foundation, and we support veterans through our therapeutic adaptive golf program. We have an outreach for young adults, and we teach them coding, with a focus on introducing STEM programming to young girls.

We also do farmer outreach in support of the USDA 2501 program, working in partnership with the University of Purdue. We're doing a lot, basically. I wear a lot of different hats. The project I'm most passionate about right now is Seed2Shirt, where we purchase cotton from African American cotton farmers; our goal is to produce our own organic cotton t-shirt line, in order to help those who have been traditionally squeezed out of the textile manufacturing industry.

Seed2Shirt is going to be a long project. It's been a lot of work so far, but I'm really excited about it, and we're working with some pretty amazing people.

Kimberly: Alright, so let's just dive right into it. What would you say has been one of your biggest obstacles, and how did you overcome it?

Tameka: For me, really, just getting everything started was the hardest thing. I know that sounds crazy, but I was afraid to start my own business. I was used to working for great people, but for a while I just didn't have the confidence to be that great person. It took about three years to get over my fear. I had many conversations, I laid out plans, I wrote out everything I would need to do -- the only thing left for me to do was start.

But once I started, I realized I can do pretty much anything I set my mind to. I've got the energy, and I've got that determination. And I'm sure some of my prior life experiences helped prepare me and toughen me up -- I went through boot camp, I was homeless for a little while, etc.

Kimberly: Fear holds us back on so many levels. You said you basically wound up just taking action and doing it, but what was it that really helped you get over the fear hurdle?

Tameka: A conversation with my mother, actually. I was telling her about what I wanted to do, I shared my doubts, and she just looked at me and said, "Baby girl, you can do it. You've already been doing it for other people. It's time to do it for yourself." So it was her belief in me that convinced me I could get my business off the ground.

After that, there was a kind of snowball effect, because two years later, I noticed there was a lot lacking in my community. There were some great nonprofits doing good work, but there was more that needed to be done. So I didn't hesitate - I talked to friends, I talked to family, and I developed a board. I started my own nonprofit, and through our first program, we were able to service over three hundred youth.

The flood gates were now open, because after this success, I was no longer afraid. I knew I could make a difference in people's lives. I knew I had this drive within me, and as long as I did the right things, made the proper plans and preparations and worked with the right people, I knew we could accomplish anything.

Kimberly: I noticed your fear kind of melted away once you started looking at yourself as a servant of the community, rather than a businessperson.

Tameka: Yeah, that's well said. I think we can sometimes get stuck in our own heads, and once you realize people, children, and entire communities have been waiting for you, it gets easier.

Kimberly: I'm not sure if you would want to go there, but earlier you mentioned homelessness. Would you mind sharing a little about that?

Tameka: Yeah. I grew up in a single-parent household, and there were always financial struggles. There were times when we didn't have a roof over our heads, but we had great people in our lives who would support us. I worried when, or if, the next meal was going to come. It just made me realize I never wanted to live like that again. I decided if I ever had an opportunity to help someone who was living like that, I would take that opportunity. I knew how hard that life was, how stressful it was, and I wanted to do anything I could to help struggling communities.

Kimberly: That's a really heartbreaking experience, especially for a child, but look what it did for you. It motivated you to give back to the community and help other struggling families.

Tameka: We know these things just make us stronger, don't they? Sometimes it's just a matter of staying still, listening to God, trusting Him, and realizing if He brought you to an obstacle, He'll lead you through it.

Kimberly: And as a result, you were able to build your own nonprofit and give back in a really profound way. Would you talk a little about your nonprofit? What exactly does it do?

Tameka: Our youth outreach programs work directly with teachers and school administrators. We host guest speaking days, career days for young adults, etc. We really focus on the technology space. We believe tech carriers are the careers of the future, and we work with organizations like Code2040, the Thurgood Marshall College Scholarship, and so on. At the end of our career days, we go into the classrooms and expose young adults to careers and career paths they might not have been exposed to. We host "hackathon" and coding days. We support teachers throughout the school year by sending guest speakers from different backgrounds that can come in and talk to the students.

Predominantly, we're focused on entrepreneurship. We have a new program focusing on farm outreach, and we're working with youth horticultural programs, we're teaching youth how to start their farms – we're doing as much as we can to help.

Kimberly: And you're teaching high school kids?

Tameka: Yes. We also work with middle and elementary school kids. Our community is primarily Hispanic and African American, and there are a lot of young adults falling through the cracks in the system. So we work with these younger kids, trying to help them stay committed to finishing their education. We want them to know there are options for them. We want them to realize there's a community out there that loves, cares for, and supports them.

We try to really form a connection with these students, so if there's an influencer they like, we'd like to show them that's an actual career. We'd like to teach them how to start down that path. Yes, it is an actual path. It's a thing people can do, and it's fun, but like anything else, it requires a lot of work to get there. So we bring speakers in to talk about the business aspect of being a social media influencer, or a blogger or something. We try to teach them it's going to take a certain level of commitment, dedication, and business skills.

Kimberly: And if you could give your younger self one piece of advice, what would it be?

Tameka: "Start earlier." Oh my gosh, I wish I would've started when I was 24, 25, but I didn't. Still, it's never too late, right? But definitely. I would tell myself to start earlier. The earlier you can get started on your true path, the better.

Kimberly: You're absolutely right. It's never too late to start. However, yes, if you had started earlier, you'd be further ahead. But it comes back to your fear of doing things. And it's not just you - no one is one-hundred percent confident when they're young.

Tameka: Also, I would say network. Networking is a very important thing. I've built my business up, I've done community work, and I've come across some truly amazing people. I've learned so much from them, they've helped me out in so many different ways, so, yeah, I really wish I would have concentrated more on networking. My business has only improved because of the people surrounding me, the ones who commit to the work we're doing.

Kimberly: Absolutely. It's the trust factor. We want to know we have a strong community to lean on.

Tameka: Exactly.

Kimberly: I love that. I'm so happy you shared that insight. That's why I love these conversations; I'm hoping they'll ignite a spark of inspiration in everyone. Hopefully they'll motivate people to start working through their fears, rolling up their sleeves, and getting started on their own journeys. Whether they're building a business, a nonprofit, or whatever - I'm really just trying to inspire people with some heartfelt conversation.

Tameka: Absolutely, absolutely.

Kimberly: You are amazing. I'm so glad we connected, and I'm glad I get to help you share your story. Thank you so much.

Tameka: No problem, Kimberly. Just getting to know you has been a pleasure, and I'm honored you considered my story important. At the end of the day, everyone is worthy of being heard. We're all trying to do amazing work out here, and you're doing really incredible things with your platform.

Kimberly: That's absolutely the truth.

Tameka: I'm just so happy to be in this space. At the end of the day, I really hope people connect with our stories and get inspired. I hope we can inspire people to start something big.

Afterword

Book 1 of this series, Goddesses Among Us, is a blessing to myself and everyone it touches.

This is an opportunity to read these conversations and allow the words to resonate within you, giving you insight and inspiration. Don't wait any longer to make a change. Allow the transformation. Give yourself permission to step into your power.

If these Goddesses could go back, this is what they would say to you, "Start earlier. Play. Tell yourself, 'I'm valuable. I'm worthy. I have meaning. I am worthy of love; not only from myself, but from everyone around me. It is safe to love. It is safe to be loved."

They would also say to you, "Don't settle for second best. Don't doubt yourself. Be grateful every day. Hang on; it's going to all work out. Never forget who you are. Follow your gut. Stay true to who you are and trust."

"It's ok to be you. It's okay to be the person that you want to be. You do not have to please everybody else. Hold on tight; it'll be a crazy ride, but you'll figure it out. Don't be afraid to feel your feelings and don't dim your light. You are unconditionally loved. You have so many other gifts, skills and talents. You haven't even tapped into them yet."

"Trust . You have great intuition. Everyone loves you. Stop going for the approval of others. Approval comes from inside you. Don't be so stubborn. Allow people to help you. You are a divinely created greatness."

"Don't waste time. Challenge your comfort zone. Don't worry. Just do what your heart tells you to do. I got you. Do not be afraid and do not underestimate your own unlimited potential!"

*"It is never too late. You can start where you are.
Be brave. Be you because you deserve it.
YOU are a Goddess!"*

Many Blessings,

Kimberly Anderson

CPSIA information can be obtained
at www.ICGtesting.com
Printed in the USA
LVHW081928161020
668841LV00010B/115